GRAND PRIX CAR DESIGN
& TECHNOLOGY IN THE 1980s

GRAND PRIX CAR
DESIGN & TECHNOLOGY
IN THE 1980s

By ALAN HENRY

1985

Hazleton Publishing, Richmond, Surrey

PUBLISHER
Richard Poulter

EXECUTIVE PUBLISHER
Elizabeth Le Breton

ART EDITOR
Steve Small

PRODUCTION CONTROLLER
Peter Lovering

PRODUCTION ASSISTANT
Wendy Owen

This first edition published in 1988 by Hazleton Publishing, 3 Richmond Hill,
Richmond, Surrey TW10 6RE.
ISBN: 0-905138-53-8
Printed by Butler and Tanner Ltd, Frome, Somerset.
Typesetting by First Impression Type Ltd, Richmond, Surrey.

Colour photography by:

Ford	– page 90
Fotovantage/Nigel Snowdon/Diana Burnett	– pages 81, 82/83, 84/85, 88/89
Dave Kennard	– page 96
Steve Small	– pages 91, 92/93, 94/95

Colour illustration pages 86/87 by Tony Matthews

Technical drawings by Giorgio Piola

Black and white photographs contributed by:

Autofoto, Gérard Berthoud, Diana Burnett, Martin Dondoz, D.P.P.I., Ferrari, Gauls GmbH, Lukas
T. Gorys, Robert Harmeyer Jr, Alan Henry, Jeff Hutchinson, International Press Agency Inc.,
Charles B. Knight, Marlboro, Marlboro McLaren Honda, David J. Martin, Phipps Photographic,
Publimotoring/Saudi Airlines, Scandinavian Racing Press, Nigel Snowdon, Sporting Pictures (UK)
Ltd, Steve Small, Sutton Photographic, Talbot Gitanes, Leslie Wright

DISTRIBUTORS

UK & OTHER MARKETS, **Osprey Publishing Limited,**
59 Grosvenor Street, London W1X 9DA

USA, **Motorbooks International,** PO Box 2, 729 Prospect
Ave., Osceola, Wisconsin 54020

AUSTRALIA, **Technical Book & Magazine Co. Pty,**
289-299 Swanston Street, Melbourne, Victoria 3000

NEW ZEALAND, **David Bateman Ltd,** PO Box 65062,
Mairangi Bay, Auckland 10

CONTENTS

INTRODUCTION

I would challenge anybody to dispute the contention that the ten years from 1977 to 1987 saw an explosion of high technology within World Championship Grand Prix racing, the intensity of which has not been approached in any other era in the sport's history. This book attempts to explain how differing strands of high technology racing car development have been drawn together by a relatively small group of extremely talented, imaginative individuals. The fruits of their labours can be seen in some of the beautifully crafted racing cars of the 1980s – the McLaren–TAGs and Hondas, Williams–Cosworths, Hondas and Judds, Ferrari F187s, Lotus–Renaults and so on.

The attention to detail and uncompromising standards which these engineers have been able to apply to their work must be regarded as one of the most positive aspects of the highly commercialised F1 environment which currently prevails. Sporting *aficianados* sometimes bemoan the arrival of multi-million dollar sponsorship, but it is all too easy to overlook the fact that it is these dollars which have helped bankroll the ambitious and innovative designs to roll out onto the circuits over the last decade.

This volume concentrates on chassis development, the province of the specialist racing car designer. Engine development over the same period is another aspect altogether which deserves to be dealt with separately by others better versed in its intricacies than myself. It is worth pointing out, however, that many current F1 engines have not been 'tailor made' in the same way as the chassis that accommodate them. With the notable exception of the TAG–Porsche turbo, the Ferrari engines and, arguably, the Judd V8, all current F1 engines have been spawned from other units, whose lineage often stems from a manufacturer's commitment to junior formulae. Hence the BMW four cylinder grew up from the German firm's F2 engine and even the Honda V6 had its roots in a 2-litre unit originally produced for the same category.

Of course, with the demise of the turbos and the switch to naturally aspirated engines from the start of 1989, we can expect to see an exciting new breed of power units which, in most cases, will not even owe their cylinder configuration to anything that has gone before. It is fair to say that those who naively believe a return to naturally aspirated engines will mean reverting to a situation where off-the-shelf customer engines dominate the scene are in for a cruel awakening.

The momentum of the sophisticated technical approach to F1 engineering which is examined in this book is unlikely to be checked by any change in engine regulations. Standards have been raised and the F1 game will continue, in the foreseeable future at least, to be played for dauntingly high technical stakes.

Alan Henry
Tillingham, Essex
June 1988

Acknowledgements:

Without the patient indulgence of several top F1 designers, engineers and team managers, it would have been impossible to accumulate all the information within these covers. My particular thanks in this connection go to Patrick Head, Frank Dernie, John Barnard, Harvey Postlethwaite, Gordon Murray, Steve Nichols, Neil Oatley, Ron Dennis and Peter Collins for their help and assistance during the period of this book's preparation.

Lotus chief mechanic Bob Dance takes a turn in the cockpit as a 'naked' type 79 is wheeled out for a test session at the Circuit Paul Ricard. This shot gives a good view of the car's slim central fuselage, compromised only by the pivot points for the front rocker arms, and wide aerodynamic side pods containing oil and water radiators. Below: Mario Andretti lifts a skirt over the bumps at Long Beach, 1979. Maintaining the seal between skirt and road was a crucial key to early ground-effect success.

Chapter 1

The chassis under the skin

When was the crucial turning-point in the mid-1970s that saw the technology of Grand Prix chassis design dropping down a gear and heading away into the ultra-sophisticated realms of super-stiff racing cars, heralding the complex era of the refined carbon-fibre composite monocoques of the 1980s? Every designer, historian and enthusiast may well come up with a slightly different answer, but there can be no doubt that when the strands of turbocharged engine development and ground-effect aerodynamics began making their mark on the Formula 1 scene, the tempo picked up dramatically. And when those two blood-lines finally mixed and interacted, the technical metamorphosis was complete.

In 1978 Formula 1 was beginning to divide itself, almost unwittingly, into two camps. The predominantly British specialist constructors, usually powering their machines with Cosworth's ubiquitous and versatile 3-litre V8 engines, prided themselves on their technical ingenuity when it came to chassis design and the subtleties of aerodynamic development. But the arrival of Renault's then rather quaint 1½-litre turbocharged V6 onto the scene the previous summer had unleashed commercial forces which were to help change the whole complexion of the sport over the next decade. Within a short time, Renault came to epitomise the motor racing establishment, aligned with the sport's governing body. Car-makers Renault were engine-orientated people and felt that the sport's competitive emphasis should reflect technical excellence in this particular area. The 'them and us' situation was destined to polarise into a series of confrontations and disputes which would call into question FISA's ability to govern the sport during the 1980s; and it almost resulted in the British teams, loyal to F1 entrepreneur Bernie Ecclestone and the influential Formula One Constructors' Association, breaking away to organise their own pirate World Championship series.

At first glance, these historical landmarks may seem far removed from the inner technicalities of Grand Prix chassis design. Yet they are, in fact, of enormous relevance. After a couple of years' persistent effort it became clear that Renault's forced induction engine had breached the ramparts of normally aspirated dominance. No matter what technical tricks of the trade the Cosworth users could come up with, the era of the turbocharged engine had well and truly arrived in Formula 1.

Throughout 1980, '81 and '82, Renault's own factory team set the turbocharged pace, although it was never clear that they had the best chassis. By now Ferrari were also firmly aboard the turbo bandwagon, but it was the 1983 alliances between Brabham and BMW and Lotus and Renault which finally mated these complex forced induction engines into innovative and truly agile racing packages. They were to be followed in quick succession by McLaren–TAGs (Porsches) and Williams–Hondas, by Lotus–Hondas and a series of Ferraris designed and developed by English engineers.

Downforce and power, both of them in prodigious quantities, became the fundamental objectives striven for by engine and chassis designers. The results of the dual quest were to be the enormous multiplication of the stresses and strains imposed on the structure of the front-running, competitive Formula 1 car in the 1980s.

As a trailer to the chassis development strand of this story we must go back to the middle of the 1970s, when Colin Chapman's Team Lotus was at its lowest technical ebb. The type 72, once a trend-setter, had its racing life much further prolonged than was intended following the failure of its successor, the supposedly lighter type 76. The next project was the type 77, initially conceived as an 'all adjustable' design which could be used with several variations of track and wheelbase.

What was to come next would, in the long term, produce a ripple-effect which lapped out to touch every other team in the Formula 1 business. Chapman sat down in August 1975 and produced a concept document which would give rise to a totally new breed of Lotus Grand Prix car. He gave the document to his Engineering Director, Tony Rudd, and directed him to set up a brand new Research and Development group to investigate the possibilities in detail and report back. Working away from the main Lotus factory, this new R & D group established its base at a former boys' boarding school called Ketteringham Hall, a mile or two down the road. Here Rudd, formerly Chief Designer at the rival BRM team, first finished his work with the Lotus Esprit road car design group and then turned his hand to his new brief.

Working closely with Rudd was a former colleague from those BRM days and a name we shall meet on several occasions – Peter Wright. A specialist in aerodynamics, Wright graduated from Cambridge and joined BRM towards the end of 1966, at the time the team was developing its abortive H-16 cylinder engine. He stayed with BRM for two years and actually toyed with the design of a 'wing car' – a crude forerunner of what would eventually emerge from the Lotus technical 'think tank' a decade later – but it quickly became clear to the young engineer that BRM was not sufficiently structured to offer him a really viable future. He quit at the start of 1969 and joined Specialised Mouldings, the Huntingdon-based experts in the field of plastics moulding who already had some involvement with motor racing.

Wright's career path over the next few years enabled him to arrive at Lotus armed with an impressive amount of experience, and this stood him in excellent stead when dealing with the aerodynamic and structural demands posed by racing car design in the late 1970s. We shall come back to his aerodynamic findings and experience in Chapter 4, but it was the work Wright and his colleagues completed on structures which assisted Lotus's F1 development through the ground-effect era and beyond.

Of course, the two projects went hand-in-hand to a significant extent. One of the most important factors behind Lotus's detailed study of structures was the necessity for a Grand Prix car to use its tyres efficiently: flexing of the suspension components or the chassis itself would clearly compromise performance in this specific area. Moreover, since the impending aerodynamic developments were certain to impose drastically increased loads on the chassis structure, this was an area where a great deal of care and forethought had to be applied.

Ironically, after Team Lotus's two-year spell in the doldrums, in 1975-76, Mario Andretti's late-season success in the Japanese Grand Prix was attributed by Chapman to the inefficiency of the Lotus 77. He told me a month or so afterwards, 'The reason Mario was able to preserve those soft compound rain tyres on a drying track surface was that they were not running at their optimum temperature because the 77's suspension didn't really permit it to use its tyres too efficiently. Ironically, in these rather unusual conditions, the car's subtle deficiency gave it what turned out to be a winning edge...'

The requirements of under-car aerodynamics and, later, turbo engines, came hand-in-hand with a major escalation in Formula 1 sponsorship involvement. Thus top team designers at last started to have the funds available for experimentation with exotic and very expensive materials. 'Whatever the technical avenues that might have been uncovered in the late seventies, the main thing that accelerated F1 technology was the availability of the necessary funds,' insists Gordon Murray. Now Technical Director at Honda Marlboro McLaren, Murray was then Brabham's top designer and responsible for a succession of interesting cars fielded by Bernie Ecclestone's team up to the end of the 1986 season.

'With the possible exception of Ferrari, few Grand Prix teams could be said to have almost unlimited technical resources,' he continues, 'and when I began working at Brabham in the early 1970s we had a very modest budget and operated accordingly strictly within it. By the end of the decade the business of slotting a Cosworth DFV engine into the back of a conventional flat-bottomed 3-litre Grand Prix car had become a practised art. You could almost do it with your eyes closed and, as far as the DFV was concerned, any worries about engine trouble could be put out of your mind. But through from the early 1970s to the early 1980s, the forces we were putting through the chassis multiplied by something like five or six times. The enormous cornering forces involved with ground effect and the strains put through the cars by turbo-power outputs made it necessary to look beyond traditional constructional methods to stiffen up the chassis, as well as considering more rigid suspension, gearbox casings and so on. That's when we began looking at honeycomb structures and began to touch on the use of carbon-fibre composites.'

Patrick Head at Williams basically agrees 'that the structures used by most manufacturers prior to 1978 were generally quite adequate for the sort of loads involved. But when skirted ground-effect cars came onto the scene, fresh demands were suddenly made on us. As an example, the loads going through our first ground-effect FW07 were more than double those that had to be sustained by FW06, our conventional Cosworth-engined design from the previous year. As an indication of our lack of concern about the strength of FW06's chassis we never got round to torsion testing one. Basically "bathtub" construction with two open box members down either side, it may have had some minor localised weaknesses, but as a rigid structure I never had any doubt that it was man enough to deal with DFV power and

Patrick Head produced the definitive 'second generation' ground-effect challenger in the Williams FW07, seen here minus engine cover. Tucking the exhaust pipes in tight towards the centreline of the car was another ground-effect priority.

the sort of download we were putting through it.'

Over at Lotus, the Research and Development team was learning a great deal about chassis rigidity as they ran static rig tests on every component destined for the new type 78 'wing car' which would eventually be unveiled just prior to Christmas 1976. The central monocoque section was very narrow, but the 78 incorporated pannier tanks on either side of a central fuel cell, so it was not until the arrival of the sensational type 79 a year later that we saw the first of the true ground-effect monocoques, an ultra-slim central fuselage, no wider than the driver's shoulders, onto which the aerodynamic side pods were hitched.

Patrick Head followed on in 1979, refining Chapman's technical philosophy to fresh levels of competitiveness with the Williams FW07, again using a monocoque with a very small cross-sectional area. That in itself brought a new challenge, ignoring the increased aerodynamic loads it would be required to sustain. 'Broadly speaking, if you halve the cross-sectional area, the torsional stiffness is reduced by between four and eight times.'

At Lotus, Chapman's design group produced an extremely light and stiff structure for the type 78, using Cellite sandwich material for the front bulkhead and side skins (Cellite comprising aluminium honeycomb material sandwiched between dural sheeting). The Lotus boss had no doubt that it would be sufficiently rigid to do the job; there had been 54 static rig tests on various of its components, so only the merit of the basic ground-effect technology remained to be proved out on the circuit.

Of course, the end product turned out to be outstanding, the type 78 winning a total of five Grands Prix during the course of 1977 (four to Mario Andretti, one to Gunnar Nilsson), but it did not represent an aerodynamic ideal and still had some shortcomings, which we will return to in Chapter 4 on aerodynamics. Back to the drawing board at his holiday home in Ibiza went Colin Chapman, bounding back into Ketteringham Hall beaming, 'right, now we've got to do it properly...' And the net result of that was the type 79.

During the course of the 1977 racing season, the type 78's Cellite construction caused a few passing problems. If the outer panel sustained damage which was transmitted through to the honeycomb core, the only really satisfactory solution was replacement. Repairs were fiddly, complicated and frequently ineffective. Chapman decided to take complete charge of the type 79 project and opted for more extensive use of aluminium sheeting, material with which he was more personally familiar.

Only the 79's monocoque floor was manufactured from honeycomb material, with all other structural panels formed from aluminium sheeting. There was an arched scuttle panel over the driver's knees, narrowing down into an extremely compact nose section. It was certainly rigid enough for its aerodynamic purposes, but there were soon to be other aspects which needed to be taken into account within the overall design equation, namely driver safety and security. That's not to say that anybody had been deliberately skimping in that area during the 1970s, but as Grand Prix racing became a more promotionally orientated business, and the acceleration of ground-effect technology triggered a cornering speed spiral, there was a growing awareness that the structures really did have to be very strong indeed to protect the drivers from the consequences of a high speed excursion off the circuit.

Over at Walter Wolf Racing, by now approaching the evening of its competitive life, designer Harvey Postlethwaite opted for a form of construction which would prove to be immensely strong and rigid. In effect using a 'scored' sheet of aluminium alloy honeycomb material, he folded the sheeting up round a series of internal bulkheads to form the Wolf WR7 which James Hunt and then Keke Rosberg drove throughout the 1979 season. It proved extremely impact-resistant, as Rosberg was to find out when he lost control at high speed during practice for the Canadian Grand Prix at Montreal, smacking the wall very hard. The car was badly damaged, but the way in which the chassis protected the driver proved highly reassuring.

In designing the Williams FW07, Patrick Head developed what was effectively a halfway house between these two concepts. Quite satisfied and experienced in the use of honeycomb materials, he based FW07 round a U-section tub formed by scoring a sheet of alloy honeycomb and folding it into the required shape, the structure then benefiting from additional fuel tank

Murray followed up the BT45 with the radical BT46, pictured in its initial abortive 'surface cooling' guise. It would later gain F1 notoriety as the 'fan car'.

top and seat-back panels, all installed in conjunction with 20-gauge aluminium inner skins. Head later found that the cockpit area of the original FW07 flexed too much, and this was stiffened by additional fillets at shoulder height on the 1980 FW07B.

Over in the Brabham camp, Gordon Murray's chassis development programme throughout the 1970s was one of the busiest imaginable, as the team's ever-changing engine supply deals resulted in his having to design cars to accommodate Cosworth DFVs, Alfa Romeo flat-12s, Alfa Romeo V12s, Cosworth DFVs again and, finally, BMW four-cylinder turbos. Gordon's first real experience with the use of composite materials had come with the pyramid monocoque BT42 he originally sketched in conjunction with Ralph Bellamy, back at the end of 1972, in preparation for the following season.

'At the time we were faced with building cars to new safety regulations which required deformable structures cladding the fuel tanks, so this system whereby an alloy outer and plastic inner skin were bonded together with a foam-injected core between them served two requirements: conforming with the regulations and making the car a good deal stiffer,' he explains.

While Chapman was blazing a ground-effect trail with the Lotus 78s and 79s, Gordon's design aspirations were compromised by the width of the flat-12 Alfa Romeo engine to which the team had switched at the start of 1976. At a time when everybody, apart from Ferrari and Ligier, was producing Cosworth DFV-engined 'kit cars', Bernie Ecclestone saw an alliance with Alfa Romeo as offering the opportunity to kill two birds with one stone. His team would benefit from the technical and financial support of a major motor manufacturer – and there was always the chance that the powerful, if thirsty and unreliable Italian engine might give Brabham an advantage over the Cosworth brigade. As it turned out, but for the intervention of ground effect, the Brabham–Alfas might well have proved the class of the field in both 1977 and '78.

Reverting to the pyramidal-shaped monocoque for his 1978 BT46, Gordon sought to take on the pure ground-effect cars with his own novel, idiosyncratic fan car. At first glance the concept of sucking the car down onto the track by means of a giant fan might seem to have come straight from Roland Emett's drawing board. It worked extremely well, however, and will be reflected on in greater detail in the section on aerodynamic development later in the book. The system was frowned on by FISA –

although not, in fact, formally banned – so Gordon was faced with the task of building his first true ground-effect car a couple of seasons after Chapman had started to set the pace with the type 78.

It was quite clear that Brabham could not build a ground-effect car based round the flat-12, so Gordon simply turned to Alfa Romeo and said, 'If you want us to have any chance at all next year, you'd better get on and build us a V12.' Alfa responded magnificently and, a few days before Christmas 1978, the first Brabham BT48–Alfa V12 rolled out of the team's factory at Chessington. Aside from its aerodynamic individuality, the BT48 was important in as much as it was the first contemporary Grand Prix car to make significant use of carbon-fibre composite panels in its monocoque construction.

In the years that followed, carbon fibre was to become one of the manufacturing cornerstones of Grand Prix car technology – and the focal point of

The difficulties experienced in packaging the Alfa flat-12 engine and a large fuel load meant that Gordon Murray was obliged to produce a conventional flat-bottomed design for the Brabham BT45, seen here at Monaco in 1977 with John Watson on board.

more speculation, doubts and muddled thinking during the early days of its F1 application than just about any other technical ingredient of recent years. From the early 1960s, government-sponsored research programmes in Britain, the USA and Japan concentrated on the development of a new ultra-stiff, lightweight material which could be employed in highly demanding areas of aerospace technology.

'The area where carbon fibre first came to my notice, and I suspect many other people's, was in the early 1970s when Rolls-Royce were using it for the first-stage compressor fans in their RB2/11 jet aircraft engine,' reflects Patrick Head, 'and that attracted a great deal of publicity, you may remember, because the end result of all these complex problems was that Rolls-Royce ended up in the hands of the receiver. As I understand it, the fans worked perfectly well and were structurally quite sound, but when a small percentage of sand or other abrasive material was introduced into the air, it stripped the epoxy resin out of the fibres and weakened the blades.

'However, my first experience of it in motor racing was in conjunction with Roger Sloman of the specialist Advanced Composites company, based at Derby, at the end of 1975 when I was with Walter Wolf Racing. We acquired the old Hesketh 308Es. They were already using carbon-fibre material in their wing structures and, of course, it was not long after that that Gordon Murray began employing it as a sort of aluminium replacement bonded into the chassis structure.'

Just as there were doubts over the structural validity of aluminium honeycomb employed in monocoque manufacture during the mid-1970s, so there were reservations about the use of carbon fibre. In the case of the former, many people felt that it would tear abruptly under sudden impacts, that the glue used for bonding the outer skins to the inner honeycomb core would break down, allowing the tubs to flex. But as far as carbon fibre was concerned, the main worry was that it would simply shatter when subjected to the destructive forces involved in a major shunt.

Paradoxically, of course, carbon fibre has no inherent strength as it is originally produced – in extremely fine filaments, each a few thousandths of a millimetre thick, and derived from a specially treated acrylic fibre, heat-treated to become almost pure carbon. These filaments are produced in bundles of up to 12,000 – known as 'tow' – and have no high-performance qualities until saturated with a small amount of resin and oven-cured at around 120°C, when they become the stiff and light material which forms the basis of current advanced composite technology.

Motor racing had been familiar with glass-fibre reinforced plastic ever since the 1950s, when it had been used in the manufacture of body panels both for racing cars and road-going sports cars. In those days the 'chopped strand' method of manufacture was predominant, that's to say that the glass-fibre strands were laid up in random directions, the theory being that this would make the resultant material demonstrate equally similar properties in all directions. However, in the manufacturing of carbon-fibre composite panels, the designer has to start with a much more precise idea of how he wants the end product to function. He can either have a bi-directional pattern, in which various weaves are specified to produce the basic strength pattern being sought; or a uni-directional product, which offers a high degree of stiffness in the direction of the fibres, allowing it to be laid in different

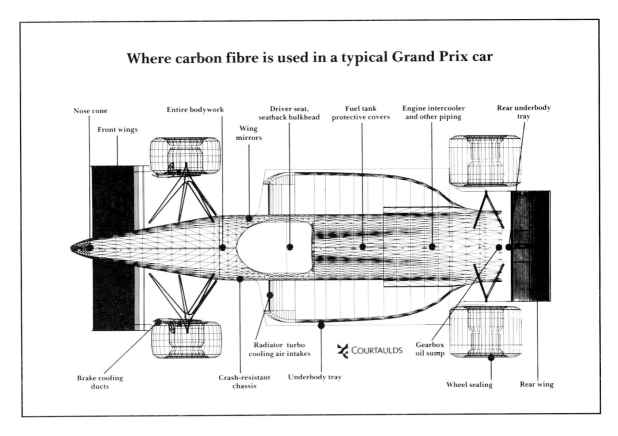

Where carbon fibre is used in a typical Grand Prix car

Nose cone

Front wings

Entire bodywork

Wing mirrors

Driver seat, seatback bulkhead

Fuel tank protective covers

Engine intercooler and other piping

Rear underbody tray

COURTAULDS

Brake cooling ducts

Crash-resistant chassis

Radiator turbo cooling air intakes

Underbody tray

Gearbox oil sump

Wheel sealing

Rear wing

This schematic drawing indicating the variety of uses for carbon fibre in the construction of a Grand Prix car was published by Courtaulds to highlight their involvement with the Tyrrell team in 1988. The car shown is the Tyrrell DG/016 dating from the previous season.

directions, bonded together to provide a component with stiffness in precisely the direction required by the engineer. This also avoids the use of excess material, and thus weight, in areas where stiffness is not really a prime consideration.

'The secret, of course,' grins Patrick Head, 'is to know what direction the load is being applied – or the areas of greatest stress and strain within a monocoque – so you can lay the fibres correctly along the anticipated load paths. What should also be remembered is that, during the early days of carbon-fibre composite in a motor racing application, there was no enormous fund of accumulated technical experience on which to draw, so, as far as Williams was concerned at least, one of the reasons for the slow introduction of such technology was that we simply had insufficient knowledge about the material. You needed to know a great deal about structures and make very confident decisions when it came to laying up those fibres in specific directions. It was real "suck it and see" stuff until 1981, when we employed Brian O'Rourke, a specialist who had previous composites experience in the aircraft industry.'

One of the basic problems with carbon fibre was that, unlike most other materials previously used in racing car manufacture, it was not isotropic (that's to say, its properties are not the same in every direction). Take a sheet of aluminium, for example: no matter how you pull, push or bend it, its fundamental properties remain the same. It is not the same with a fibrous material. As a simple example, think of a block of wood. It's very difficult to fracture *across* the grain, but relatively easy to split *along* the grain. In

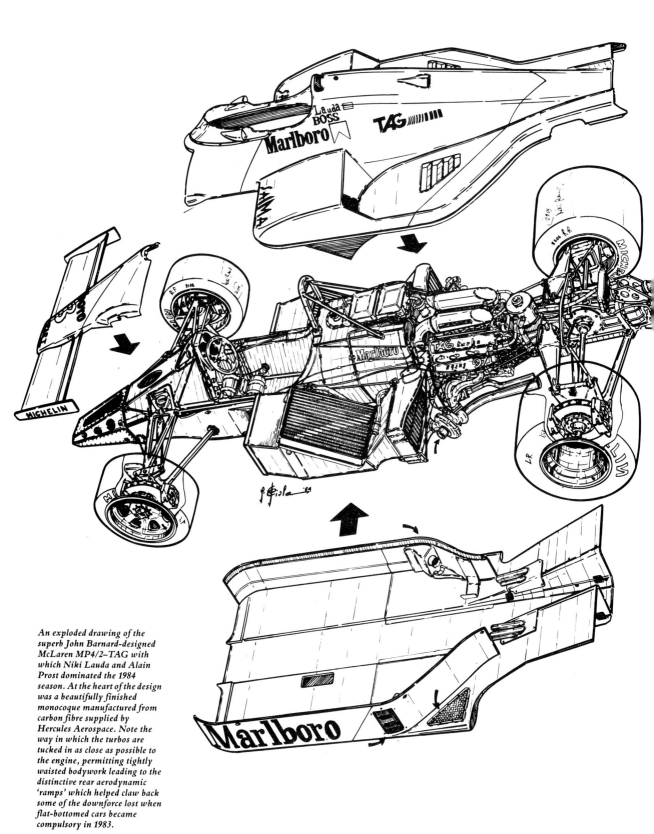

An exploded drawing of the
superb John Barnard-designed
McLaren MP4/2–TAG with
which Niki Lauda and Alain
Prost dominated the 1984
season. At the heart of the design
was a beautifully finished
monocoque manufactured from
carbon fibre supplied by
Hercules Aerospace. Note the
way in which the turbos are
tucked in as close as possible to
the engine, permitting tightly
waisted bodywork leading to the
distinctive rear aerodynamic
'ramps' which helped claw back
some of the downforce lost when
flat-bottomed cars became
compulsory in 1983.

22

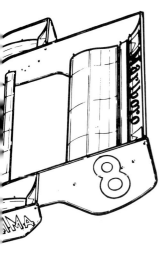

essence, that analogy explains why it is of such crucial importance to ensure that the carbon fibres are laid in the correct direction for the stresses involved.

By the end of the 1970s most leading Grand Prix designers were toying with carbon fibre, to a lesser or greater extent. Gordon Murray and Patrick Head continued to pursue relatively conventional avenues of monocoque manufacture over the next few years, so it was the catalyst of the McLaren/Project 4 amalgamation towards the end of 1980 that gave rise to the first all carbon-fibre composite monocoque F1 car, John Barnard's sleek McLaren MP4.

Barnard, who by this stage had already developed a very respectable track record with design work for McLaren in the early 1970s, had just designed the superb Chaparral 2K in which Al Unser had led the 1979 Indy 500 until its gearbox failed. Later that year he was approached by Ron Dennis of Project 4 Racing and the two men talked over a potential F1 design project for the future. Ron, his team now well practised in the F2 and Pro-car arena, felt ready to make the move into F1. John had some pet theories about manufacturing an all carbon-fibre composite chassis – and their joint ambitions eventually gelled when Marlboro nudged the existing McLaren management in the direction of an 'amalgamation' with Project 4 at the end of 1980.

Project 4 was already moving towards the manufacture of Barnard's carbon-fibre composite prototype when the merger with McLaren was finally announced; in other words, by hook or by crook, they were going to take it into F1 anyway. But now they had the finance and the resources to get on with the job in style. Barnard, originally apprehensive about what he saw as the problems of 'technical management by committee', which he anticipated would result from the partnership with McLaren, none the less threw himself into the task with gusto, appreciating the resources which would now be to hand.

However, in the short term, he found himself rather disappointed over the reception his ideas for a carbon-fibre composite monocoque were receiving in the UK. 'To be honest, there was really not a great deal of enthusiasm or interest at all,' he reflects, 'because the big concerns who were capable of doing the work simply did not have the capacity for such specialised components. It was only when a friend in the USA, Steve Nichols, suggested a company in Salt Lake City might be interested that we actually made some progress. The company involved was Hercules Aerospace and, one Friday evening, I returned to the factory from another abortive trip to a British supplier and sat in the office as Ron called these people and attempted to make contact with somebody who could give us a decision. Eventually we found the right man, he gave us the nod and, almost immediately, we flew out to Salt Lake City to explain what our requirements were and did the deal.'

Hercules, who were very active in carbon-fibre technology, were involved in ambitious projects such as missile rocket motors. The deal with McLaren International – as the team was now called – was that Barnard designed the car, Hercules made the required panels and they were then flown to Britain for bolting and glueing together to form a light and rigid completed structure. Barnard explained that there were also secondary benefits to be derived from this method of construction, namely a dramatic reduction in the number of components required to make the monocoque.

He estimated that as many as fifty aluminium sections would be needed to manufacture a conventional chassis, but the carbon-fibre design employed a mere five main mouldings in addition to the outer shell.

The McLaren MP4 marked an historic turning-point in 1980s Grand Prix racing. Not only was it the first pukka carbon-fibre composite chassis in the business, but it signalled what was to come from McLaren International. The team had slumped spectacularly in its efforts with the enormous, complex and unreliable ground-effect M28, only slightly salvaging matters with the unspectacular, if improved, M29, but the new regime would take it back to the top within another three years.

Meanwhile, Colin Chapman was preoccupied with a wholly different set of problems. His answer to rock-hard suspension developments, and his

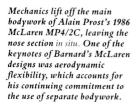

Mechanics lift off the main bodywork of Alain Prost's 1986 McLaren MP4/2C, leaving the nose section in situ. *One of the keynotes of Barnard's McLaren designs was aerodynamic flexibility, which accounts for his continuing commitment to the use of separate bodywork.*

response to the failure of his own aerodynamically complex 'wingless' type 80, was to attempt to separate the aerodynamic loads from the chassis itself. The battles he was to have with the sport's governing body over the acceptance (or not) of this concept were to sap his enthusiasm for motor racing as one of the last unfettered frontiers of technical development. (This is an aspect which will arise again in the chapter dealing with aerodynamics.) But it was the monocoque construction of the twin-chassis Lotus 88 which really kindled everybody's interest.

At about the same time as carbon-fibre materials were being developed in the aerospace industry, the Du Pont Chemicals company in the USA came up with a new man-made material called Kevlar. It could be made much more straightforwardly than carbon fibre, based as it was on an organic polymer,

Riccardo Patrese on the grid at Zolder before the start of the 1982 Belgian Grand Prix in his 'naked' Brabham BT50–BMW. The panels over the driver's legs were from carbon fibre, but designer Gordon Murray still retained alloy honeycomb for the main constructional panels.

similar to a high-grade cellulose-like flax, but about four times stronger. It did not rot and deteriorate like flax, and was about one-third the stiffness of carbon fibre, as well as being significantly less expensive.

Commercially available carbon-fibre/Kevlar cloth, pre-impregnated with the crucial epoxy resin, was employed in the manufacture of the 88's monocoque. At this point there were two basic methods by which a carbon-fibre monocoque was assembled and cured into its finalised, rigid shape. Either one started with carbon-fibre/Kevlar cloth and simply brushed on the epoxy resin by hand, before leaving the cloth to cure for up to 48 hours; or pre-saturated material was used, which could first be shaped the way the designer required and then 'cured' by exposure to heat and pressure in an autoclave pressurised oven.

It was Peter Wright who suggested that the 'anti-tear' qualities of Kevlar would be ideal to complement the already acknowledged basic qualities of carbon fibre, and he developed a constructional method which was extremely straightforward and efficient. The basis for the 88's monocoque turned out to be a flat sheet of carbon/Kevlar skinned sandwich material, within which was a honeycomb filling of Nomex paper-foil. The panel was about eight feet square and the epoxy resin was ladled on by hand, before being rolled in evenly all through the sheet.

Lotus left the sheeting to cure chemically but, before the resin had totally hardened, pre-positioned apertures were cut into the structure in order to take mounting bobbins for engine pick-ups, side-pod fixings and suspension mounting components. The whole panel was scored and literally folded up round dummy internal bulkheads, the edges bonded and taped together, and the whole structure finally left to cure. The tub was then stiffened by the insertion of aluminium bulkheads which were bolted into place to provide additional support for the engine and suspension mountings. The result was an enormously strong and durable structure. This system of chassis manufacture served Lotus splendidly well for five seasons and was only superseded for the 1986 Lotus 98T when Gerard Ducarouge opted for a moulded one-piece monocoque on the last of the Renault-engined cars.

The increased use of carbon fibre offered designers a really reliable means of ensuring that their latest breed of ultra-narrow section monocoques remained suitably rigid and secure, but there were still designers reluctant to go the whole hog and commit themselves to such manufacturing techniques *in toto*.

Gordon Murray: 'At the end of 1979 we switched back to Cosworth power with the BT49 after an abortive season with the Alfa Romeo V12, by which time I think it's fair to say that our monocoque designs contained pretty well a 50/50 split between alloy and carbon-fibre panels. But over the next year or so we had a couple of big accidents with the car and the frontal section absorbed the energy very badly, so I must say I panicked a bit and raised the prospect with Bernie Ecclestone about destroying a complete car in a controlled crash test before extending the use of carbon fibre any further through the car.

'Eventually we did the tests with a BT49 at BMW's test centre in Munich and the results told us an enormous amount about the "crashability" of carbon fibre. After that we began to use more and more of the stuff, but I've always been extremely conservative and ultra-conscious of driver safety in

26

The Williams FW08 was essentially a further derivative of the successful FW07 series, incorporating many changes, notably the high-sided alloy honeycomb monocoque and the adoption of pullrod suspension to clean up the airflow to the ground-effect side pods.

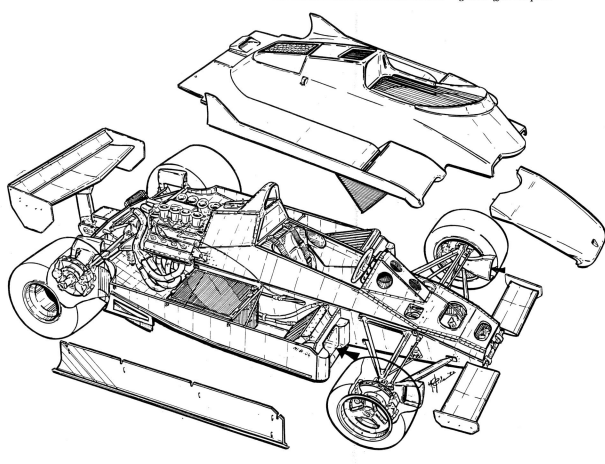

my designs, so I regarded carbon fibre with considerable caution from the outset. I watched other people get involved, some of whom clearly did not fully appreciate what they were doing, and there were some horrific crashes with cars falling apart.

'We learned an enormous amount from Roger Sloman's Advanced Composites company, but at the end of the day there was no substitute for bringing the manufacturing process in-house and teaching ourselves. Carbon fibre had been used in aerospace applications for some time, but the requirements of an aeroplane and a racing car are completely different from a structural point of view, not least of which is that an aircraft requires a certain degree of flexibility for it to be safe. And, of course, people don't design aeroplanes to deform and absorb energy progressively as they run into mountains…'

The last of the front-line F1 teams to climb aboard the carbon-fibre bandwagon was Williams, Patrick Head waiting until midway through 1984 before finally deciding the team had sufficient knowledge and, perhaps even more importantly, adequate control over the manufacturing process, to feel really confident.

Head, of course, felt the same way as Murray when it came to questions of driver safety. He knew that a good aluminium sheeting/honeycomb monocoque, made to high standards, could have qualities of impact resistance of an impressively high standard. 'There were aspects of the behaviour of certain carbon-fibre composite/honeycomb materials which I wasn't terribly impressed about,' he reflects, 'notably the way in which you saw things like skirt boxes exploding during the ground-effect era when a lot of people were using those awful foam-cored honeycomb panels which all looked pretty disastrous and didn't really impress me a great deal.

'In addition, we had two massive shunts with FW06 and FW07 respectively in which the monocoques stood up extremely well. The first was at Watkins Glen in 1978 when Alan Jones's car broke a hub shaft, the second in 1980 when Carlos Reutemann went straight on at Copse and slammed into the vertical sleepers on the outside of the corner in an impact which must have been somewhere in the region of 120 mph. I was impressed and gratified about the way in which the monocoque stood up to the impact.

'Now although I'm in business basically to build what is, hopefully, a quicker racing car than those from our rivals, if we have an accident in which a driver gets seriously damaged, I would like to think that we have used our best efforts to produce a car which is as strong as possible. Having said all that, I think I was probably a little bit asleep and rather on the slow side developing our own composites department here at Williams.'

Patrick also talks about his essentially cautious attitude in another important sense. 'I've always tried to take a somewhat practical approach towards the cost involved in producing a Formula 1 car. I've had a tendency to say, "This may be a little bit nicer, but it's going to cost ten times as much, so we won't do it." I try to keep costs down to a reasonable level. Some years ago I remember we drew up some test panels which were to be made by a French company for impact test purposes and, when we got the quote in, I was shocked by the fact it seemed like telephone numbers. As a result, I got a little bit wary about dealing with sub-contractors from this point of view and concluded that we would accumulate sufficient expertise to do the job

In 1983 the Gustav Brunner-designed ATS D6 broke new ground by being the first F1 car to dispense with separate upper bodywork, the smooth surface of its carbon-fibre monocoque licked by the airstream.

in-house before we embarked on a full programme of carbon-fibre monocoque construction.'

Having said all that, Head has no doubt that an aluminium honeycomb structure could be made to be as stiff and safe as a carbon-fibre chassis. 'But it would have to be much heavier. Anyway, the biggest limitation of an aluminium structure is that it can't be handled in the same way as carbon-fibre cloth. One major benefit of working with carbon fibre is that the monocoque can be made to provide the outer body shaping without the need for separate bodywork which necessarily limits the cross-section of the chassis. That philosophy was first demonstrated in the 1983 ATS D6 which was really not a bad effort and quite an attractive car.'

Notably slow and sceptical to pick up the carbon-fibre gauntlet was Ferrari, of course, who in 1981 fielded possibly the second turbocharged engine – after the Renault – to join in the Grand Prix game. As usual, Maranello continued in its belief that the engine was the heart of any racing car and the first 126CK chassis was hardly a nimble greyhound, even though the gifted Gilles Villeneuve manhandled it to victories at Monaco and Járama that season. However, there was to be a crucial catalyst which helped drag Ferrari out of the technological dark ages: the recruitment, midway through 1981, of Harvey Postlethwaite, the former Wolf F1 designer whose folded aluminium honeycomb chassis had proved so impressively impact-resistant a few years earlier.

Harvey's arrival was to spark off a gradual programme of technical updating, which would eventually give rise to the first of the carbon-fibre composite F1 Ferraris making its race debut in the summer of 1983. For 1982 Postlethwaite used a new aluminium honeycomb construction, materials for which were supplied by the Belgian division of the American Hexcel company, this organisation also carrying out bonding operations on panels which were too big for

Progress at Maranello. Harvey Postlethwaite's Ferrari 126C2 design for 1982 was based round an alloy honeycomb monocoque built from sheets 'folded up' round internal bulkheads.

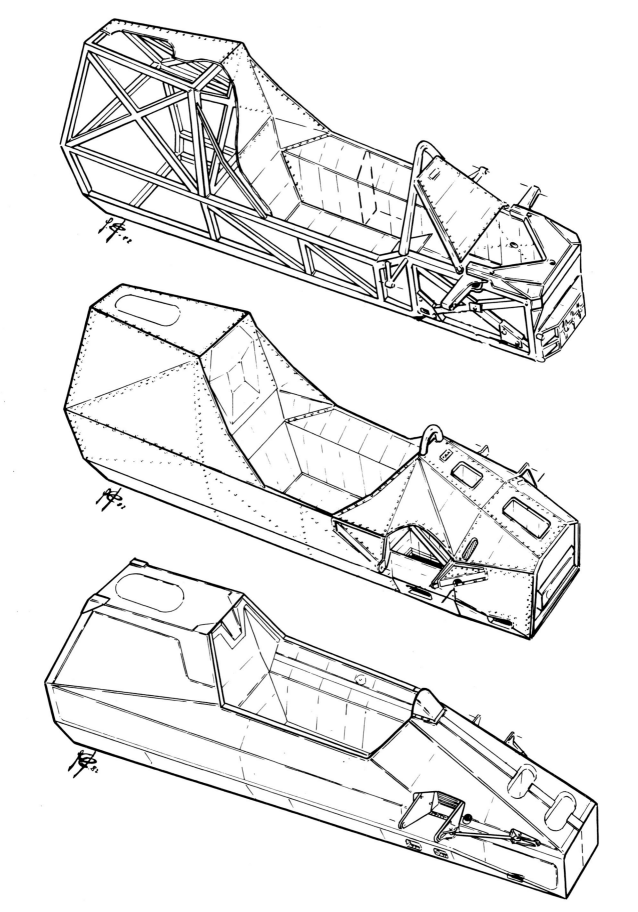

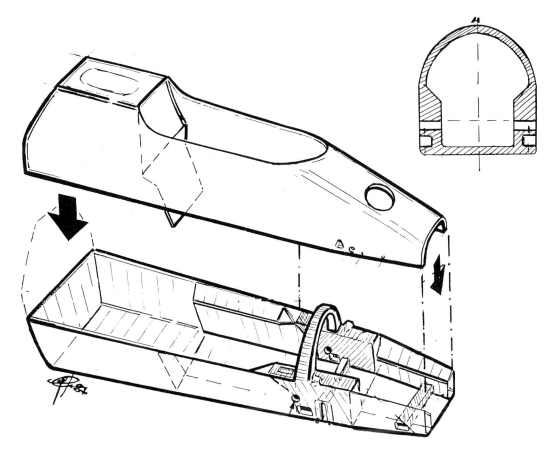

The evolution of the Ferrari 126-turbo series chassis can be seen from these three Giorgio Piola drawings opposite, starting with the small-tube frame overlaid with alloy sheeting of the early cars and progressing through to the 126C2 alloy monocoque which immediately preceded the team's first carbon-fibre machine.

Above: **The Ferrari 126C3 monocoque was a two-part carbon-fibre construction, bonded together at waist level.**

the Ferrari factory to deal with. The assembly methods were a distant variation of the Lotus 'score and fold around' method. Maranello laid two 'U'-shaped channel sections on their side and then bonded them together down the centre line to produce the completed tub. For maximum driver protection the monocoques were high-sided, and Ferrari claimed this new monocoque structure to be almost five pounds lighter than the 126CK from the previous year.

At the end of the 1982 season Formula 1 was shaken by a major technical rule change, banning the use of aerodynamic underbodies and, essentially, insisting on flat-bottomed machines from the start of the following season. By this stage the design team at Maranello had completed a ground-effect 126C3 test car, fitted with a new longitudinal transmission and constructed round one of the existing aluminium honeycomb monocoques. This then had to be scrapped and rethought to conform with the new regulations, so while the racing team kicked off the 1983 season with flat-bottomed 'conversions' on the existing cars, the design department, by now installed in brand new premises a stone's throw from the old factory and backing onto the Fiorano test track, finalised its first carbon-fibre composite chassis. Interestingly, when it came to installing an autoclave sufficiently large to accommodate a Formula 1 monocoque, Mr Ferrari instructed that it should 'be big enough to accommodate a 400i'. That was pretty far-sighted stuff, of course, although the GTO and F40 would be the first Ferrari road cars to benefit from the new technology.

While the C3 development was getting under way, Ferrari's first use of composite materials was encompassed in the GTO's design, an up-to-the-moment illustration of how cross-fertilisation between racing and road cars works in the 1980s. In this case the carbon-fibre composite materials were not used in any

33

Gordon Murray's first all-carbon-fibre Brabham design was the abortive low-line BT55, here seen minus all body panels. Its ultra-low cockpit exaggerates the apparent size of the BMW engine's Behr intercooler.

structural, stress-bearing panels, but simply in the fire-proof bulkhead between the passenger and engine compartments, plus the bonnet. In the former case, this large panel also contributed to the strength of the monocoque assembly when bolted into the shell, as well as doing a fine job insulating the occupants from the heat and noise of the turbocharged engine bay. The decision to use carbon fibre for the bonnet panel was reached after high-speed tests with a metal bonnet demonstrated that the thrust of air tended to distort it until it popped open; to make one sufficiently strong out of the same material would have exacted too much of a weight penalty, so a carbon composite substitute proved ideal for the job.

Back on the F1 front, the C3 was taking shape and eventually made its first public appearance in pre-British Grand Prix tyre tests at Silverstone. Made out of carbon composite reinforced with Kevlar '49', its tub was moulded in two parts, the upper and lower mouldings being bonded together with magnesium bulkheads positioned in between them. Just like the ATS D6, which slightly preceded it, the 126C3's nose and cockpit shape was formed by the outer skin of the monocoque itself, with only a circular access hole and a hatch in the nose allowing mechanics access to the footwell section of the car. The 126C3 qualified on pole, first time out, at Silverstone and helped the marque to win its second successive Constructors' title.

Gradually, throughout the 1980s, Gordon Murray's Brabhams adopted more and more carbon-fibre composites in their construction. When it came to the task of designing a brand new car for 1983 to take the BMW M12/13 four-cylinder turbocharged engine, Murray still opted for an aluminium outer-panelled tub with carbon-fibre inner walls, a technique he sustained right through to 1986 when he rounded off his Brabham design career by producing the low-line BT55, the single most ambitious – and unsuccessful – concept of his entire career.

The Brabham BT54 was the last Brabham design to have an alloy honeycomb outer skin, but the section over the driver's feet was already made from carbon fibre.

By 1985, Gordon's BT54 was the last contemporary F1 machine to retain an aluminium outer monocoque skin, but his innovatory technical concept for the following year called for a completely new tub moulded entirely from carbon-fibre composite. We shall look into the theoretical advantages and practical problems which surrounded the disappointing low-line BT55 in Chapter 4, but it was a significant car from a historic viewpoint representing, in effect, the last CFC 'doubter' coming across completely to embrace the new manufacturing technology.

Murray, now with McLaren, remains stoical when he reflects on the BT55 and its shortcomings. 'It was really a question of going the whole hog when we didn't have time to get every aspect of the car's design totally sorted out,' he says thoughtfully. 'What I had completely underestimated was the length of time it would take to build a completely new, all carbon-fibre composite car from the ground up, with transverse transmission, lay-over engine and a brand new monocoque package which was no more than 16½ inches high. If I'm honest with myself, I have to say that we really needed the best part of another six months and that sort of luxury just wasn't available to us.'

Patrick Head, meanwhile, had made the switch to all carbon fibre in 1985 after a season grappling with the unloved (by its drivers, anyway!) FW09/9B range, which were the first Williams–Honda turbos. Keke Rosberg was adamant that the car had insufficient chassis rigidity and that's why it was always prone to understeer, a viewpoint Head tends to reject.

'I don't look back on 09 as the greatest car we ever designed, but, equally, I don't believe it was ever as bad as it subsequently got tagged. That understeer problem that Keke was always complaining about was more a product of the engine's abrupt throttle response rather than any inherent defect in the chassis.' Clearly, Rosberg had a bee in his bonnet on this particular subject…

We will see in Chapter 4 on aerodynamics how the relentless pace of development quickly resulted in designers regaining the lost ground-effect downforce by conventional means, ensuring that, by the turbocharged engine's heyday in 1986–87, cars which were capable of developing in excess of 1200 bhp (in pre-4-bar boost limiting valve trim) could not only produce top speeds of 220 mph, but also generate cornering load factors in excess of 3-G. Therefore, since the fundamental handling characteristics of a racing car are affected by the way in which the chassis and suspension components interact with each other, it became an absolute prime requisite that the monocoque should have tremendous stiffness.

The first carbon-fibre composite Williams FW10 chassis, built prior to the 1985 season, demonstrated considerable improvements in stiffness over its aluminium honeycomb predecessor, the FW09. For example, in the cockpit bay area a 65 per cent increase in torsional stiffness was measured for the same weight of component. Using the outer shape of the monocoque as its 'bodywork' makes for a complicated moulding, which was manufactured in two stages. The outer skin was cured at maximum autoclave pressure of 7-bar (100 lb/sq. in.) while the honeycomb and inner skin were cured at half this pressure. These two elements were then assembled using a cold-set adhesive before being drilled to accept the relevant mounting points for suspension components and the attachment of other major parts.

Of course, while a great deal of energy has been devoted to the refinement of techniques for the use of carbon-fibre composites in the manufacture of monocoque structures, there are inevitably other areas of the current F1 car where this technology is of considerable value. The nose-box, for example, must now be a deformable structure demonstrably able to absorb

The long nose of the McLaren MP4/4 reflects the 1988 regulation requiring that the driver's feet should be located behind the front-wheel centreline.

A Benetton B188 nose section ready on the rig for the FISA crash test at Cranfield, February 1988.

a 39 kJ frontal impact while restricting damage to that area ahead of the driver's feet. Several teams have carried out much of this work on the large pendulum rig at the Cranfield Impact Centre, teaching them a great deal about the impact performance of composite materials and, at the same time, going a good way towards allaying the doubts expressed by some people about the suitability of CFC in motor racing applications.

Undertrays for today's GP machines are also carbon composite in construction, the requirement being that they are light, rigid, easily removable and capable of sustaining any amount of 'kerbing' on the part of undisciplined drivers. They have also, in the recent past at least, been required to survive next to a red-hot turbocharger as well as being subjected to exhaust gases. Carbon-fibre composites are ideal for the job. Similarly, rear wings must be light, easily adjustable and capable of being fitted by a single mechanic. A typical contemporary F1 rear-wing assembly must be capable of carrying aerodynamic loadings of around 100 times its own weight. Again, carbon-fibre composites provide the solution.

In twenty years, Formula 1 chassis construction technology has leap-frogged from the time when tube-frames were still to be seen forming the basis of some of the most competitive cars in the business, through to an era where complex aerospace technology has become a fundamental cornerstone of the F1 car's gestation period, long before it has seen the competitive light of day. Moreover, the acceleration of this technology must be set against the usual F1 timescales – which allow precious little leeway for any production hiccup, let alone design error.

Chapter 2

The right suspension at the right time

Look back to the rear suspension set-up of the Lotus 78 and you can pin-point a minor, if significant, turning-point in contemporary Grand Prix car design. The superb under-car aerodynamics of Chapman's first wing car were compromised by a conventional approach to the rear suspension lay-out. At the front the coil-spring/dampers were tucked into niches in the outer monocoque wall. At the rear, however, the set-up was less tidy. Massive fabricated uprights, inclined coil-spring/damper units and exhaust pipes cluttered the area between the wheels. Put simply, front and rear didn't seem to match up.

A season later, the elegant chassis configuration of the Lotus 79 heralded a subtle change of emphasis. The rear suspension was tucked away close to the engine/gearbox package, only top rocker arms and lower wishbones protruding into the ground-effect venturi which swept right through to the rear of the car. Suspension design was still an important element in the over-all package, but the 79's layout underlined the fact that other considerations also had to be taken into account, not least of which was the aerodynamic influence any particular layout exerted on the car as a whole.

Thirty years ago the transverse leaf spring was only just giving way to the familiar double wishbone/coil-spring arrangement which remained a con-sistently popular configuration throughout the 1960s and at the beginning of the 1970s. It was a layout which offered the designer a number of basic advantages, including relatively low unsprung weight, permitting the wheels to react to irregularities on the track surface much more quickly. Such systems were also very light and easy to adjust because they were so straightforward and accessible.

Initially it was the accepted practice to mount the co-axial spring/damper units between the bottom of the suspension upright and the top of the chas-sis, but eventually a trend developed to move them completely inboard, activated by extensions to the upper wishbones which operated, effectively, as rocker arms. Side radiators and side pods generally made it aerodynami-cally more desirable to keep the spring/dampers mounted inboard and, of course, the advent of ground effect made it an absolutely top priority. Dur-ing this period of development, the fabricated rocker arms grew in size, strength and cross-sectional area, imposing an increasing effect on the car's aerodynamic performance as well as adding considerably to the all-up weight. An alternative was clearly required.

Gordon Murray pioneered pullrod suspension on the Brabham BT44, using semi-inboard coil-spring/damper units and double wishbones as early as 1974.

Back in 1974, Gordon Murray turned his thoughts to this matter while finalising the design for the second new car he produced during his tenure as Brabham Chief Designer. The pyramid monocoque BT42 featured outboard coil-spring/dampers sitting in the airstream, but for the 1974 BT44 Murray repositioned the springs and evolved a pullrod activation system which he originally had in mind for a Formula 750 special.

Murray had hoped to continue racing himself at a modest level after leaving South Africa for England. He eventually discovered that the 750 Club's little sports car formula offered an absolutely ideal technical playground. 'I'd been forced to abandon the idea of racing when I found it so difficult to get a job, and discovered how expensive everything seemed to be over here,' recalls Murray. 'But then I stumbled on this fantastic little formula where there were virtually no chassis design restrictions, so I designed and began to make my own monocoque chassis. I spent about a month fiddling around with the concept, trying all sorts of levers and linkages to keep the system in tension and compression.

'The problem with a rocker arm was that, as the suspension loads gradually increased over the years, designers were having to make the rocker arms bigger, stiffer and stronger to prevent them flexing, but no matter how much you beefed them up, there was still the problem that they were acting like an undamped transverse leaf spring – which simply went against the grain.

'I had worked out all the geometry and stresses in my 750 design and transferred them all into the BT44. As it happened, the pullrod system turned out to be ideal for the subsequent generation of ground-effect cars. Pullrod systems later gave rise to a further variation with pushrod activation of the inboard coil-spring/dampers, although, in practical terms, there is virtually nothing to choose between the two systems. It eventually comes down to a question of pure packaging, how the physical shape of the front end of the monocoque affects the positioning of the spring/damper unit. In my estimation, the only appreciable difference is that the pullrod system is about 10 to 15 per cent lighter than the pushrod because the former is in tension, while the latter is in compression.'

The pullrod system is where the rod runs from the upper outboard end of the wishbone into the bottom of the inboard mounted spring/damper unit. On bump, as the wheel moves up, it pulls the rod with it, acting on the spring by means of a small rocker. A pushrod system is precisely the reverse of this. The rod goes from the outboard end of the lower wishbone to the top of the inboard mounted spring/damper which is again activated by a small rocker arm. On bump, as the wheel moves in an upward direction, it pushes the rod upwards. It's as straightforward as that.

Because the suspension loads involved were very direct, and there was no requirement for that large rocker arm, it was possible to utilise wishbones which were considerably thinner and therefore had less adverse effect on the car's aerodynamics. Also, the spring/damper units could be tucked away inside the monocoque, which could still be quite narrow at the front end. With rocker-arm suspension, the pivot point has to be a long way out into the airstream in order to exert adequate leverage; that factor necessarily produced another undesirable aerodynamic byproduct in the form of a large and rather ungainly fairing.

Whereas Brabham were first on the scene with a pullrod arrangement, it

Cluttered. The Lotus 77 was used, in effect, as a test bed for components in preparation for the type 78 wing car. The untidy rocker-arm suspension, with vertical spring/dampers mounted outboard, was in stark contrast to what was to follow in 1977.

Tyrrell's 1985 Renault-engined 014 displays a classically straightforward pullrod front suspension layout with unequal-length wishbones.

40

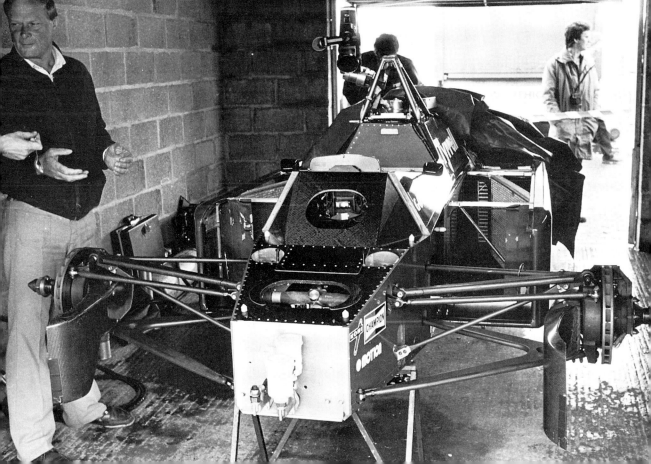

was John Barnard at McLaren who first evolved the pushrod system for his revamped flat-bottomed MP4/2C at the start of the 1983 season. Barnard recognised the fact that the pullrod system was significantly lighter, but it had the slight disadvantage that it operated the heavier end of the shock absorber which contained the oil. Initially he gave consideration to reversing the whole arrangement, inverting the shock absorber so that the oil was up at the top and the lighter end was at the bottom. That didn't work, so John came up with the pushrod configuration.

Rocker-arm activated inboard suspension systems survived on even some of the fastest cars in the business through until the end of 1981, after which there was a gradual realisation that this was not the answer in the ground-effect era. When Williams brought out the FW08, with its pullrod front suspension, all they were in fact doing was producing an updated 07. 'In some ways, you know, the first FW08 was effectively FW07 "E",' recalls Williams aerodynamicist Frank Dernie. 'We discovered from our wind-tunnel research that quite a lot of lift was being generated by those rocker arms and rocker-arm fairings on the front suspension. That's why we designed a new car with pullrod suspension, although at the time you could hear people saying that pullrod suspension was fundamentally better than what had gone before. In my view, it was no better at all – any loaded component on a racing car should be in tension or compression, if possible – it merely enabled us to improve the car's

Harvey Postlethwaite cleaned up the 126C2 design with pullrod front suspension, later transferred to the sleek C3, seen here with René Arnoux working it hard at Monza, 1983.

aerodynamics and perhaps save some weight. But we wouldn't be talking about much, only very small percentages.'

John Barnard's 1983 McLaren MP4/1Cs featured pushrod activation of their inboard spring/dampers, replacing the previous year's rocker-arm system.

Interestingly, Dernie believes that such subtleties as suspension geometry are 'virtually meaningless' in today's F1 environment. 'Some designers seem to go to enormous amounts of time and effort calculating suspension geometry, fabricating elaborate structures to hang out on the gearbox casings, for example, to achieve what they believe to be critical pick-up points. On other cars there will be no evidence of such efforts being made. So you can conclude that there may be two designers who have come to totally differing conclusions in this specific area. One says it's crucial, the other that it's not worth the weight.'

Suspension development was by this stage becoming little more than an adjunct to the effectiveness of the car's overall aerodynamics, but there were other detailed aspects to consider. Now that suspension loads were all being transmitted inboard, anti-roll bars changed quite dramatically: they became extremely compact and activated by levers which are designed to produce varying degrees of resistance when subject to torsion. By the early 1980s most cars had cockpit controls to adjust the anti-roll bars, a development which really only benefited the driver at relatively low speeds in ground-effect machines. Once the car began gaining a worthwhile head of speed, and the aerodynamic forces really came into play, the car's handling characteristics were totally dominated by its aerodynamic performance.

Ultimately, of course, suspension development, in what might be termed the 'conventional' sense of the word, rolled to a standstill in the mid-1980s. Once designers had concluded that aerodynamic considerations made it essential that coil-spring/dampers should be mounted inboard, the details of the suspension installation became just one more aspect of the overall packaging and integration of the design, a subject which will be examined in more detail in Chapter 5 on 'Integrating the design'. Here we have to consider what was undoubtedly the most fascinating and challenging area of suspension design in the 1980s: the evolution of what came to be called 'active' suspension systems. They are still very much in their infancy as these words are being written.

Back in 1981, Colin Chapman's Research and Development group were thinking hard of ways in which they could engineer the team's F1 cars out of the regulatory mess which FISA had inadvertently imposed on the Grand Prix game. In the wake of the ban on sliding-skirt F1 cars, the necessity for a constant ride height under the new fixed-skirt rules had helped spawn that absurd breed of rock-hard go-karts, while the suspension lowering systems, as trail-blazed by Gordon Murray at Brabham in an attempt to get round the 6 cm ground-clearance rules, ushered in a season of technical frustration and irritation. Either the rules needed to be changed, or there had to be a way round the bone-jarring rides, structural strains and total lack of conventional suspension movement which this truly dreadful breed of racing cars had produced.

Lotus's development of what was to become its active suspension system was born out of a programme instigated to develop an instrumentation system by means of which the team could record and monitor under-car airflow during those pioneering years with ground effect. Peter Wright became very involved with the Cranfield Institute of Technology and grew intrigued with the possibilities offered by the Cranfield's Flight Intrumentation Group. At the time they had a variable-feel aircraft control system under development, for installation in British Aerospace's Hawk trainer. The purpose of this was to simulate the feel of just about any other aircraft currently flying, thereby dramatically widening the experience available to trainee pilots.

Cranfield engineer Dave Williams suggested it would be possible to produce an 'active' suspension system from this flight control technology, based round the variable-resistance hydraulic jacks which were at the centre of the aircraft control system they were developing. Peter Wright instantly realised the implications and suddenly found himself embroiled in what he was to describe as 'certainly the most exciting project I had ever been involved with up to that point'.

Put simply, the new system would work in much the same way as the human muscular system relates to impulses from the brain – in this case, a central computer. A steel spring/damper system has a measure of deflection but, as Wright puts it: 'Legs are not springs and, when the brain senses a variation in the ground surface on which they are walking, it instantaneously compensates for it.' That was what Lotus and Cranfield sought to develop into the new 'active' system.

Wright's biggest challenge was working out a means of programming the hydraulic activators to react and compensate in exactly the right way to whatever input the system received. In 1981 the team built an original Turbo Esprit road car as a test bed, to see whether the system was feasible or not. During early testing, both Nigel Mansell and Elio de Angelis were quick to appreciate the long-term possibilities offered by the system. In 1982 the go-ahead was given to build an active suspension F1 development car, this being completed a matter of days before Colin Chapman's sudden death in

Nigel Mansell was the guinea pig who did much of the initial testing with the Lotus active suspension system when it was fitted to the Ford–Cosworth-powered type 92, which is seen here struggling in the 1983 Brazilian GP at Rio.

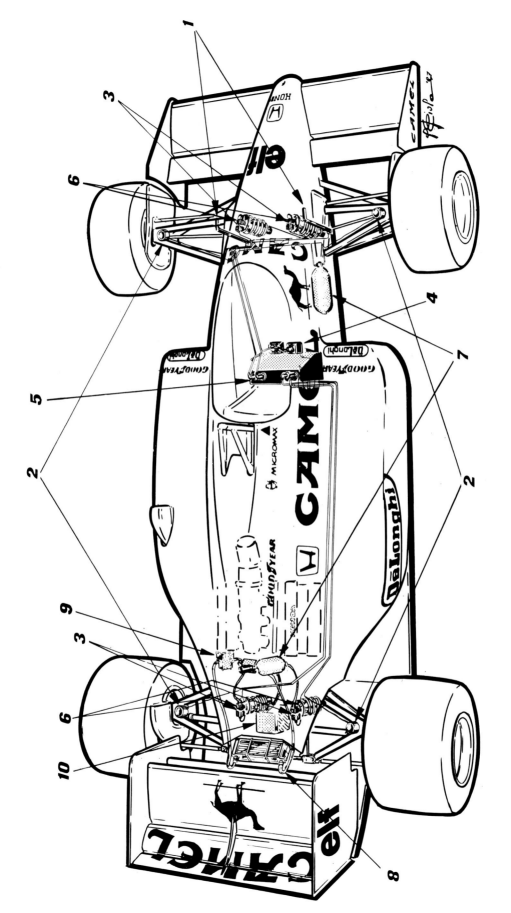

December. Then, following on close behind that tragedy, FISA's rule-change stipulating flat-bottomed F1 cars from the start of 1983 rather diluted the initial reason behind the development of the active system.

However, Team Lotus kicked off the 1983 season running one Renault turbo-engined 93T for de Angelis plus a Cosworth DFV-powered Lotus 92 for Mansell. By this stage so much money and effort had been expended on the active system that Team Lotus decided to race it in a couple of Grands Prix, just to see if it worked. Mansell therefore drove the 'active' 92, its hydraulic activators having no back-up conventional steel springs, at Rio and Long Beach. The car was heavy, unreliable and generally uncompetitive, so no spectacular race results were produced. But Wright and his colleagues were now satisfied that they could package an active system into a Formula 1 car and make the whole thing function successfully.

Of course, the active suspension system was a Group Lotus patent, and while technological collaboration between the road and racing car operations had flowed freely while the Chapman dynasty controlled both arms of the empire, things changed very significantly after Colin's death. Today, General Motors owns Lotus, so that the Formula 1 team (which remains a private entity controlled by the Chapman family) had to come to a commercial arrangement with the road car company prior to using the active suspension system on its cars in 1987. The result was the active Lotus 99T–Honda in which Ayrton Senna and Satoru Nakajima started off the 1987 season with such high hopes.

By the time Team Lotus came to adopt the active system in 1987, development of the original concept had progressed quite dramatically. The Mark III 'active' also had the benefit of secondary 'get you home' back-up springs, onto which the car settled in the event of an hydraulic failure. These were good enough to enable the driver at least to struggle back to the pits and not be forced to abandon the car out on the circuit. In fact, they turned out to be sufficiently serviceable for Senna to battle home to third place in the German Grand Prix at Hockenheim after a race fraught with technical problems, including just such an hydraulic failure.

The interface between the electronic control systems and hydraulic activators on the 1987 active suspension system was provided by five Moog variable-flow valves, one of which was fitted to the outlet on the lightweight aerospace pressure pump, driven by a mechanical coupling from the tail of the Honda V6's left-hand exhaust camshaft. The other four were on each suspension corner of the car where they converted tiny electronic impulses into hydraulic movements.

Ensuring that the system was insulated from random input caused by vagaries in the road surface, but at the same time making sure that it responded to input required or instigated by the driver – such as acceleration, braking or cornering – proved extremely difficult. The end result, though, was an extremely pleasant car to drive. Senna's World Championship challenge was blunted by other shortcomings of the 99T's design, such as its inferior aerodynamic profile, with all the resultant implications for fuel consumption *vis-à-vis* the lower drag profile of its Honda-engined rival, the Williams FW11B. The active suspension system was generally adjudged a plus-point, although the nature of the beast meant that it was virtually impossible for Team Lotus to derive the maximum benefit from its complexity within the

confines and pressures of a Grand Prix racing season.

Beneath the driver's seat on the 99T was positioned the system computer which received a continuous flow of information on the car's motion and control input from the driver. These were detected by a number of transducers, accelerometers and potentiometers situated around the car, including those which sensed lateral and longitudinal acceleration and were also housed beneath the seat.

While the active Lotus was stationary in the pits, its onboard computer could not only be plugged into an engineer's keyboard, which could be used to extract read–out data from the brain beneath the seat and examine how the car had been behaving and responding, but the extracted data could also be fed into a large-capacity computer installed in the pit garage, which gave scope for more detailed analysis. In addition, the technicians could use the plug-in keyboard to make adjustments to the onboard computer's programme, resetting ride heights, and fiddling with damping or any other aspects of the suspension's behaviour.

The great advantage of the pit garage computer was that the engineers no longer had to rely on the driver's description of a handling imbalance. It was now possible to call up the relevant part of the memory bank, select whatever graphic or numeric display was required, and get down to the business of analysing the problem in detail. Yet, ironically, here was part of the fundamental problem. The computer enabled so much information to be drawn out, it being possible to overlay a lap on the screen with just about every element of the car and the engine's performance, that the actual business of getting back onto the circuit and pressing on with the job in hand – qualifying for the grid – almost found itself in danger of being overlooked. The sheer volume of input consistently ran at such a daunting level that, in the field, Team Lotus could do little more than scratch the surface when it came to analysing it in any depth.

Of course there was always going to be a flip-side to the use of active suspension and, in the case of the Lotus, this had to be added to the car's aerodynamic shortcomings. The system added between 10 and 12 kg to the all-up weight of the car and, in addition, driving the hydraulic pump lost some power from the Honda V6, which also contributed to taking an edge off the 99T's performance. But the overwhelming feeling in the team was that the system was potentially such a major benefit it was too good to ignore. The first time Ayrton Senna tried it he became so excited about its possibilities that the programme became incorporated into Team Lotus's 1987 plans from the outset, rather than being kept in the background as a sort of option which the team could work towards using, once the basic 99T had been sorted out. Most people agree that the first Lotus–Honda was better for having active suspension than it would otherwise have been, but the team did not continue with the project in 1988.

Lotus, of course, was not alone in considering such a system. Even before Peter Wright forged his link with Cranfield, at the start of the Lotus system's development period, the British car component company Automotive Products was toying with the concept of an 'active' suspension system. It was based broadly on the Citroen ride-levelling systems which had long made the otherwise unremarkable French family saloons such superbly relaxed devourers of long distances over bumpy road surfaces.

Variety is the spice. This array of 1988 F1 suspension detail reveals a wide variety of approaches. Gustav Brunner's Rial (top left) *has shock absorbers lying along the lower edge of the monocoque.* Centre left: *Ligier's JS31 has inboard rear springs activated by pullrods. Benetton's B188* (lower left) *uses pushrods to operate its deeply concealed spring/dampers.* Below: *the rear end of the reactive suspension Williams FW12, showing off its transverse six-speed gearbox.*

The needle nose of the Tyrrell 017 (top) incorporates small spring/damper units mounted on the front bulkhead, similar to the AGS JH23 (above), but pullrod-activated.

AP was just cruising quietly along in the slow lane with this project, unpressured by the demands of a high-tech motor racing programme. Then, in 1985, the Williams F1 team began to show an interest, its objective, of course, being an application for its Grand Prix cars. AP engineer Bob Pitcher, in charge of the active-ride system, liaised closely with Patrick Head on the project for a couple of seasons before AP eventually decided that it wasn't really interested in continuing its support for such a scheme and withdrew. Pitcher continued off his own bat and at his own initiative, while Head and his R & D colleague Frank Dernie got down to the practicalities of developing the system for possible use on the F1 car.

In the Williams camp Nigel Mansell was less than effusive about the system from the start. He had memories of tests with the early Lotus 92 active suspension and could recall occasions when the computer 'hiccupped' and

The front suspension of the 1985 Williams FW10, showing pushrod suspension and unequal-length wishbones.

Nelson Piquet on his way to a commanding victory in the 1987 Italian Grand Prix at Monza at the wheel of a Williams FW11B equipped with 'active-ride' suspension.

sent the wrong messages to the hydraulic activators. The result wasn't something he particularly liked recalling so, as far as the Williams system was concerned, he was happy to leave its development to team-mate Nelson Piquet. Of course, this was right up the Brazilian's street, a nice behind-the-scenes testing project which might add up to something that could offer him a major performance advantage on the circuit. And so it proved.

Nelson spent the best part of a season, on and off, working away, helping develop the active-ride system. Shortly before the Italian Grand Prix at Monza he ran a test at Imola, over the same distance as the San Marino Grand Prix which had taken place there earlier in the year. Ironically Nelson had not taken part in that event, being obliged to sit it out on the sidelines following a major practice shunt, but Mansell had won commandingly in the other Williams. When Piquet turned in a time at Imola that was a minute faster than Nigel had managed in the race proper, it was clear to the Brazilian driver – and to the rest of the team – that the active system was ready to race. Nelson used it at Monza – and won.

Running closer to the track, Nelson's active-equipped FW11B was able to generate more downforce and, consequently, the 'conventional' rear-wing angle could be reduced. Thus the winning Williams–Honda had an edge in straightline performance, yet still retained the downforce necessary to perform competitively through Monza's dauntingly quick corners. Ironically, Piquet won after a routine stop for tyres – but Senna's 'active' Lotus was just hanging on at the front of the field, running through non-stop, when he got slightly off-line at the Parabolica and slid onto the sandy outfield, dropping behind the Williams to finish second as he wrestled the 99T back onto the circuit again.

The Williams active-ride system had an accumulator which was charged by an hydraulic pressure pump driven in the same way as the Lotus system – from the tail of the left-hand exhaust camshaft on the Honda engine. High-frequency reactions induced by the road surface were handled by a strut and gas-spring sphere, mounted in sequence, at each suspension corner; each one also interacted with an electronically commanded valve which allowed pressured hydraulic fluid in and out of the strut in order to control its length.

A rheostat mounted in parallel with each strut then signalled changes in length to a central computer which, acting upon this input, was then

programmed to respond by sending the correct message to the hydraulic valve blocks. These fed the gas-spring spheres in which the pressurised fluid was separated from the gas by means of flexible diaphragms. As the fluid displaced the membrane, so it served to raise or lower the gas pressure on the other side of the system.

The Williams system was less complex than the Lotus active suspension, having fewer sensors on the car, and having been developed purely for competitive motor racing purposes. The Lotus system has, of course, always had a parallel road car application which has made it more wide-ranging in its ability to cope with the sort of surface variations one could reasonably expect to encounter in a frost-damaged English country lane, but would be less likely to come up against on a first-rank international racing circuit.

The reduction of motion stress on the drivers is less of a priority with the Williams system; its prime function is to produce a consistent ride level which will promote aerodynamic stability and increase the amount of consistent downforce available. The system exacts a small weight penalty and involves minuscule power sacrifice of about 5 bhp. Clearly the team has great faith in it, and the new Judd-engined Williams FW12s with which Nigel Mansell and Riccardo Patrese are campaigning the 1988 Grand Prix season have been fitted with it from the outset.

Active suspension development is an area which other teams are currently investigating with cautious optimism. As we reach the end of an era which has been dominated by the prodigious and unfettered power outputs afforded by turbocharged engines, and the massive performance advantages they have offered to some teams become a thing of the past, further developments in the subtle area of suspension technology are certain to absorb more designer-time in the next few years.

Moreover, whether or not there is any direct partnership between specific teams and road car manufacturers, the development of these systems will increasingly be seen to have benefits for road cars in decades to come. As Peter Wright puts it, 'I'm pretty sure that in 100 years' time all cars will have active suspension. In fact, there are plenty of indications that many cars will have active suspension by the early to mid-1990s. Initially it may be on specialist vehicles, top of the range cars, but eventually I feel it will spread more widely through volume ranges.'

A familiar sight. Changing ratios on a Hewland-based transmission: Toleman team, 1982.

Chapter 3

Transmitting the power

Over the past decade, Grand Prix car transmissions have become an ever more complex and crucial element of the overall package. Twenty years ago, the gearbox was an off-the-shelf component one purchased, more often than not from Hewland Engineering, the specialist manufacturing company based at Maidenhead, and the adoption of the Ford–Cosworth DFV engine as F1 racing's almost universal power unit meant that any designer contemplating a move into F1 knew pretty specifically the parameters within which he was working. The power output of the DFV ranged from only 370 to 470 bhp – over a fifteen-year span. Once you had opted for a certain gearbox and transmission, therefore, it would last you quite some time without undue problems.

However, the advent of the turbo era changed all that. While various Grand Prix teams developed their own subtle modifications to what were essentially 'productionised' gearboxes, the massive power increases that came hand-in-hand with the turbos meant that transmissions were suddenly being subjected to dramatic levels of additional loading.

Specific installation requirements, such as the need to mount suspension pick-up points on the gearbox, have prompted various designers over the years to manufacture their own special outer casings, but even as late as the 1986 season every British F1 team bar Brabham was using Hewland gears inside their transmissions. The development of Hewland's current FGB gearbox, which still forms the basis of many contemporary F1 systems at the time of writing, began as long ago as 1969 when the first FGA gearbox was produced.

Attractive propositions because of their rugged, compact construction and sheer versatility, development through to the heavy-duty FGB gearbox, which was first made available in 1979, was a logical and constant process of refinement. The FG400 was eventually superseded because of the extra stresses and strains imposed by the advent of ground effect, and the trend towards outboard rear brakes and inboard mounted suspension called for a much slimmer casing altogether.

The need to change ratios quickly 'in the field' has meant that most racing transmissions have evolved with their gear clusters protruding from the rear of the differential, and it is only relatively recently that weight distribution considerations have prompted major and consistent departures from this route. Two memorable exceptions to this, of course, were Robin Herd's

A Hewland-based transmission with the gear cluster to the rear: Toleman TG184, 1984

notorious Alfa Romeo–spawned inboard box on the unloved March 721X, and the later, much more successful transverse gearbox on the 1975 Ferrari 312T. The product of Mauro Forghieri's clever thinking, this lasted well into the 1980s on Maranello's racers.

The Hewland FG400 differential also featured limited self-locking capability, any loss of grip by one wheel allowing it to spin freely until the limit of the differential was reached, at which point it locked to provide much improved traction. The later FGB was manufactured with a standard Hewland self-locking device which became an increasing priority in the late 1970s, to combat lack of traction out of slow corners.

Conventional differentials transmit torque through the differential cage to bevel gears which split the torque equally between the two driveshafts. In wet or otherwise slippery track conditions, if one wheel loses grip it begins to spin, unsettling the car quite dramatically. The next potential

hazard occurs when that spinning wheel regains its grip. It will do so suddenly, immediately transmitting unwanted torque through to the other wheel, prompting an unexpected and unsettling disruption of the car's equilibrium. A self-locking differential will overcome this problem, imposing a braking effect on the driveshaft when that wheel is turning faster than the other.

By the end of the 1970s, the five-speed FGB gearbox was being purchased by most Grand Prix teams, effectively in component form and adapted/modified to the individual requirements of the various constructors. Transmission development has always been prohibitively expensive for most Grand Prix teams and Hewland's specialist ability has served a crucial need over the past three decades in every international racing category. However, there will always be constructors who want to move one step ahead of the rest, the late Colin Chapman being one of them. The Lotus boss had a preoccupation – some would say obsession – about producing his own gearboxes – a quirk which to some degree compromised the development of his trend-setting ground-effect type 79 during the 1978 Grand Prix season.

McLaren's MP4/4–Honda uses a Weismann-developed three-axis gearbox to reduce driveshaft angularity.

The neat tail-end treatment of the 1986 Ferrari F186, showing its transverse gearbox and the diffuser panel beneath all the suspension arms.

Back in 1957, Chapman's first Lotus 12 Formula 2 car had been imbued with an inherent streak of mechanical unreliability, owing to his insistence on developing a purpose-made racing gearbox. This relied on drop-gears to set down the drive from the front engine, keeping the car's centre of gravity as low as possible, the drive entering the gearbox on one shaft and leaving it on a second, lower one. Five gear sets were used. Those on the output shaft were actually splined to that shaft, leaving those on the input shaft free to rotate round a sleeve containing a set of dog-rings which would slide out to engage the centre of the individual gears. With a sequential, motor cycle-style gearbox, it was extremely unreliable. Not for nothing did it quickly become known as 'that wretched queerbox...'

At that time Lotus had been incorporating limited slip differentials, manu-factured by Zahn Fabrik Friedrichshafen in Germany, and it was to 'ZF' that Chapman turned for a new transmission with the advent of the Lotus 21. Throughout the 1960s Lotus experimented with Hewland and Colotti trans-mission variations, while a BRM gearbox was naturally used for their unsuc-cessful interlude with that company's H-16 engine in 1966. But Lotus stayed with ZF right through to the early days of the Lotus 49, when dire failures prompted by the massive torque developed from the new Cosworth DFV engine, allied to the impractical nature of the German gearbox's fixed final drive and intermediate gear ratios, forced Chapman to abandon the ZF trans-missions in favour of the quick-change ratio attractions of Hewland products, at the start of 1968.

Chapman used to refer to Hewland's gearbox as a 'collection of old man-gle gears', an expression born out of a blend of affection and frustration. His conviction that it must still be possible to produce a better tailor-made gear-box package than that available 'off the shelf' from a supplier, whose wares were also used by Lotus's rivals, was to bug him for the remainder of his life. Despite many set-backs, he would never stop experimenting on this front.

When the time came to pension off the superb Lotus 72, early in 1974, designer Ralph Bellamy's new type 76 was originally unveiled with an ambiti-ous electronic clutch system. The car attracted a great deal of media attention at the time with its 'four-pedal control' and button atop the gearchange knob, theoretically enabling the driver to use the 'conventional' clutch pedal only when leaving the starting grid. Thereafter, he could employ a left-foot braking technique to steady the car and minimise pitch changes as it was 'set up' for the corners. The button on the gearchange activated an hydraulic system of clutch withdrawal, but while the team's number one driver, Ronnie Peterson, origi-nally enthused about the system, it did not work.

It was back to the Hewland route for another four years, but Chapman wouldn't rest. The type 76 almost wrecked Team Lotus's fortunes, prompt-ing a major reorganisation and revamped approach and, when Chapman set up the Research and Development group, whose long-term efforts resulted in the unlocking of ground-effect aerodynamics on the Lotus 78 and 79, he also chose to revive the 'queerbox' concept, handing it all over to Ralph Bellamy to reassess the potential for a new transmission system. Bas-ically, Chapman was looking for a much smaller and lighter gearbox than anything Hewland could produce. Earlier experience with the 'queerbox' had shown that the gearwheels were extremely durable, but the dogs employed to engage the ratios sustained tremendous wear, so now the

61

The complex rear-end package
of the 1979 Ferrari 312T4
included a transverse gearbox
with spring/dampers
immediately behind in an
attempt to keep the airflow from
the side pods as uncluttered as
possible.

system was to have various major refinements.

The gearwheels revolved round the hollow input shaft, each gear containing four small balls which were knocked into engagement with the appropriate gearwheel by means of a bobbin which ran within the shaft itself. The system was modified to provide a non-sequential gearchange, something which most F1 drivers had long become accustomed to by the late 1970s.

Lotus beat a path to ZF's door for the limited slip differentials, while that other German company, Getrag, was also recruited to assist with the project. They were particularly fascinated by the system's potential, as they had some experience with a similar ball-engagement system from a much earlier 'bubble car' project.

The new gear engagement system did not involve either dogs or meshing, so it was now theoretically possible for drivers to dispense with the clutch on the up-changes, although that assumed they could always time things perfectly. This followed, in part, the philosophy behind the original 'four-pedal' 76, namely that minimising pitch changes on the approach to corners was a major priority, more so than ever now that Chapman was unlocking the secrets of ground-effect aerodynamics.

Mario Andretti raced the new Lotus/Getrag/ZF gearbox only once, at the non-Championship 1978 Silverstone International Trophy meeting, thereafter persuading Chapman that his title aspirations should not be compromised by continued experimentation with this system. Bearing in mind the chassis advantage the type 79 was about to demonstrate over its rivals, it was totally the correct decision for Mario to abandon the new gearbox. He raced to the Championship in a car fitted with a 'standard' Hewland package.

His team-mate Ronnie Peterson, however, found himself assigned to development work 'in the field' with the new gearbox, although it did not take long for events to develop into a highly predictable pattern. Peterson started out GP weekends experimenting with the new gearbox, its final drive invariably gave trouble and, for the second day's qualifying, his car would be revamped with a Hewland transmission. This was not always as straightforward a task as one might think, for the type 79 weight distribution changed dramatically, depending on which gearbox was fitted, forcing Ronnie to start second qualifying at the wheel of what was effectively a new car. It was not a routine calculated to produce the best results and, within a few races, Peterson's car appeared with the Hewland package fitted from the outset.

By the end of the year Chapman was so preoccupied with the business of taking ground-effect technology into its second generation that the new type 80 reverted to the familiar Hewland FGA gear cluster, albeit enclosed in sleek Lotus casing which split at 90 degrees to the centreline of the car rather than longitudinally, as on the standard Hewland casing. The complete gearbox itself was in the rear portion, leaving the clutch housing and oil tank in the forward section.

Chapman's gearbox experimentation had been typical of the man's attitude and approach to the business of F1 design work. Other people's off-the-shelf products were not really what he wanted, so he left no stone unturned to give his team that extra advantage not available to his rivals. The fact that the systems he adopted were over-complex in many ways, and certainly unreliable, was in his view no reason for failing to explore them as far as he could.

Meanwhile, over at Ferrari, Mauro Forghieri spent much of the latter half of 1974 overseeing the design and development of a compact transverse gearbox which would be positioned ahead of the rear axle-line on the forthcoming 312T Formula 1 car. This was the car to be raced by Niki Lauda and Clay Regazzoni the following year. Of course, such an attempt to move the main mass of the car as far forward as possible, in the interests of improved handling, was nothing new. In 1972 Robin Herd had tried a similar approach in the development of what turned out to be the catastrophic March 721X.

Encouraged by Ronnie Peterson's performance in finishing second behind Jackie Stewart in the 1971 title chase, Herd decided to refine the 711 design which had scored second-place finishes in five Grands Prix the previous summer. Peterson had been invited to drive one of the factory Alfa Romeo T33 V8 sports cars in the 1971 Watkins Glen Six Hours endurance race; he reported to Herd that he was impressed with the gearbox, mounted ahead of the rear axle, in the Italian car. March had already been involved with Alfa for the supply of engines on an irregular basis the previous year, so Herd took the matter from there.

Alfa supplied March with the necessary gearbox components, but the car simply never worked properly from day one. A combination of poor weight distribution and a chassis which didn't get the best out of the Goodyear tyres, to which the team had changed at the start of 1972, augured badly for the whole project. Peterson kept faith with the concept, despite the fact that the 721X was plagued with dire understeer and lack of grip from the outset. To this day, Herd regrets that he failed to take much notice of the team's new cub number two driver, who stepped out of the car after practice for the Spanish Grand Prix at Járama and told him, 'No way will this car ever work!' Robin admits he pooh-poohed the novice youngster. Shame, really; his name was Niki Lauda...

Ironically, it was Lauda who benefited from the technical renaissance which began with the Ferrari 312B3 in 1974, leading to the transverse gearbox 312T the following year. The B3 suffered from abiding understeer, no matter how the chassis was set up, but when Lauda first tried the 312T at Ferrari's Fiorano test track, the Austrian realised just what an improvement the new car actually was. Its balance was superb and the car had a near-neutral feel to it, no matter how much fuel was aboard.

The gearbox, of course, was one of the crucial keys to this improved handling. The gear cluster lay ahead of the axle-line with the shafts at right-angles to the centreline of the car. Power was taken by means of bevel gears to the input side of the box, final drive being by means of spur gears. A removable plate on the side of the casing allowed access in order to change ratios and there was a cast bridge-piece fitting across the top of this neat little unit which provided pick-up points for the upper end of the still outboard-mounted coil-spring/damper units.

This transmission system proved extremely rugged and reliable, lasting out the flat-12 cylinder naturally aspirated Ferraris to be fitted, in beefed-up form, to the first of the 126C turbocharged cars at the end of 1980, by then revamped to offer a choice of either five or six speeds.

Of course, this transverse Ferrari gearbox is quite heavy and complicated, but its compact rectangular dimensions mated up nicely to the flat-12 cylinder engine with which it was originally paired. The bell-housing is integral with the gearbox casing and accommodates such ancillaries as the starter

64

motor, clutch and various castings to provide for suspension and rear-wing pick-up points.

Ferrari's transverse box was not an ideal package around which to develop a ground-effect chassis, but then neither was a flat-12 cylinder engine. Nevertheless, the combination proved just the ticket in 1978, winning five races in the face of opposition from the trend-setting ground-effect Lotus 79s, and again in the following year when Jody Scheckter took the title at the wheel of a 312T4.

In fact, the unit survives to this day in six-speed form, although it was scheduled to be scrapped at the end of 1982 when Harvey Postlethwaite was evolving the Italian team's 1983 ground-effect F1 challenger. A longitudinal transmission was developed with the obvious aim of ensuring that the aerodynamic venturis under the rear of the car were as wide as possible. Then the 'flat-bottom' rule knocked that idea on the head, just as it had wrecked Gordon Murray's BT51 project and ruined John Barnard's hopes of making the McLaren–TAG MP4/2 the definitive ground-effect contender.

Meanwhile, by the time Ferrari's transverse box had appeared on the scene, developments to individual Hewland transmissions were just starting on an *ad hoc* individual team basis. Over at Brabham, Gordon Murray began examining the FG400's lubrication system during the 1974 season, with a few ideas of his own.

'We did a great deal of work on that gearbox during the first year of the BT44 programme,' he recalls, 'starting with our own dry-sumping system which included a new rear casting with an oil pump built in. It collected all the oil and repumped it through the gear clusters. It made a big difference – at that time the "standard" Hewland only had splash lubrication.'

The basic Hewland lubrication system involved oil being ducted through the pinion shaft which was drilled with a succession of tiny holes, enabling the oil to pass out through the needle rollers into the gears. By the end of 1975, McLaren engineer Alistair Caldwell managed to bring a personal theory to fruition with the development of the first FG400-based, six-speed transmission. This, it was felt, would allow the then current M23s to maximise the performance offered by the rather peaky power delivery of the team's DFV engines prepared by Nicholson–McLaren.

Caldwell's idea involved adapting what was originally reverse gear on the layshaft into a first gear, repositioning reverse on the back of the bearing carrier and oil pump, driven by a revamped input shaft inside the main cage adjacent to the crown wheel and pinion. McLaren also had to design a new oil pump because the original Hewland one would not fit within the repackaged transmission. Used on James Hunt's McLaren M23 throughout his successful onslaught on the 1976 World Championship, the Caldwell-conceived six-speed Hewland was the first of several such adaptations which would surface on the F1 scene within the next few seasons.

As far as transmission development in the early 1980s was concerned, the spiralling power outputs from the new breed of turbocharged F1 engines meant that gearboxes would have to be beefed up quite dramatically to stand the strain. But there were still some interesting experiments connected with attempts to maximise the now obviously dying potential of the naturally aspirated brigade, and these involved an element of ingenuity in the gearbox department.

In 1977, Robin Herd had toyed with the aerodynamic advantages of a six-wheeler F1 chassis based on the March 771, using a third axle and final drive tacked onto the back of the existing chassis, but using four small rear wheels to do the driving. As was usual at the time, March did not have the budget to progress this concept beyond the prototype phase. However, fours years later, Williams designer Patrick Head mulled over a development of that concept in his mind at a time when the Didcot team was fighting a determined rearguard action against the turbos, using their John Judd-developed 530 bhp DFVs.

Head calculated that the contemporary large F1 rear tyres accounted for something like 40 per cent of the car's aerodynamic drag, so the six-wheeler layout looked pretty promising in the team's wind tunnel. The new rear end was centred closely round the two-wheel drive car's rear axle-line, so the leading rear axle was placed some four inches ahead of the regular position, the driveshafts being angled forward to cope, while the third axle was driven by an additional final drive tacked on the back, in similar style to the March.

Hewland offered Williams some assistance with the transmission development, drawing on experience with the March six-wheeler which was now being hillclimbed on the British scene by leading exponent Roy Lane. Immediately following the 1981 Las Vegas Grand Prix, Williams and Head tried using the six-wheeled FW07 'D' as their ace card in attempting to persuade Alan Jones to revoke his recent decision to retire from the cockpit. Rather than head straight home to Australia, following his winning drive at Caesar's Palace, Jones was prevailed upon to backtrack to the UK where he tested the six-wheeler prototype at Donington Park. Jaded with F1 he may have been, but Jones was impressed. The FW07 'D' accelerated away from a standing start like a rocket, with virtually no wheelspin at all. The Australian ace was tempted, but he decided to stand by his original decision and quit – for the time being.

Problems packaging the rear aerodynamic underwings prompted Patrick Head to rethink his concept, producing a second prototype based round an FW08 monocoque. However, four-wheel drive and six-wheelers were included on the same 'prohibition' list which saw the end of ground effect at the start of the 1983 season, consigning the six-wheelers to the history books as tantalising 'might-have-beens'.

The requirements of ground-effect aerodynamics led the Brabham team up an interesting, if unproductive, alley during the 1981 season with the development of a brand new transverse gearbox for the BT49–Ford Cosworth which, up to that moment, had been relying on an Alfa Romeo transmission casing equipped with Hewland ratios. That year's Long Beach race marked the first public appearance of a gearbox/final-drive unit produced by American specialist Pete Weismann, whose previous experience had largely been confined to transmission work on Can-Am and Indy cars. The new Brabham gearbox could be fitted with either five or six speeds, the gear shafts running transversely across the car as part of Gordon Murray's desire to produce the ultimate ground-effect design by keeping the underside of the chassis as smooth and uncluttered as possible.

The directional change from the crank axis to the gear shafts was by low friction, straight-cut bevel gears, and on the right-hand side of the casing was a detachable plate through which the gear cluster could be withdrawn

in order to facilitate ratio changes. This transmission was packaged in conjunction with inboard-mounted coil-spring/damper units, activated by rocker arms, mounted vertically behind the ultra-slim transmission. The oil tank, feeding a lubrication system common to both engine and gearbox, was mounted within the bell-housing.

'The whole package was extremely light, rigid and compact,' recalls Murray, 'but we really needed more facilities and personnel to develop it to its optimum pitch. Ideally, we would have required a separate factory with about a dozen technicians on the project full time to make it work properly. Gearbox development is a very time-consuming and expensive business.' And it was not destined to become any less so as the turbo era arrived in F1.

Murray had originally intended to use a derivation of this transmission on the ground-effect BT51 he was planning for the 1983 Grand Prix season. But, since this project had to be scrapped with the advent of the 'flat-bottom' regulations, yet another gearbox had to be produced for the new BT52 'dragster'. Nelson Piquet used this to win the 1983 Brazilian Grand Prix – on its maiden outing.

Throughout 1983, and into '84 and '85, the Brabham five/six-speeder was progressively beefed up, with technical input largely from Weismann, who had been retained by the team as a consultant. With upwards of 1000 bhp being developed by the BMW-turbo in qualifying trim, the transmission proved extremely marginal on several occasions, but it held together long enough to enable Nelson to win the 1983 World Championship.

In 1986, Weismann was again called upon to produce a new gearbox for the striking low-line Brabham BT55, the car with which Gordon Murray hoped to re-establish his reputation as an innovative and trend-setting arbiter of F1 design. Unfortunately, as we saw in Chapter 1, the overall complexity of the BT55 eventually defeated the team's best efforts to unlock its potential in the time available during a hectic racing season.

Reclining the BMW engine at an angle of 72 degrees in the chassis obliged Weismann to produce a bevel-drive transmission which incorporated an 'overdrive' ultra-high seventh gear. This, it was hoped, would enable the BT55 to produce startling acceleration and enviable top-speed capability. Unfortunately, it was not really possible to pinpoint precisely where the car's fundamental deficiencies lay (although rival designers certainly had their ideas!). The whole project amounted to a spectacular failure which – in a bitterly tense and acrimonious atmosphere – helped seal the fate of the Ecclestone/Murray/BMW triumvirate.

Meanwhile, over at Williams, Patrick Head and his colleagues had evolved a six-speed, Hewland-based transmission which in 1983 would allow the FW08Cs a final fling against the turbo brigade. Keke Rosberg and Jacques Laffite managed to hang onto the fastest turbos on quick circuits by using every ounce of steam developed from the Judd-modified Williams DFVs. So it proved at the Belgian Grand Prix at Spa, where the two FW08Cs hung gamely onto the tail of the front-running turbos, Keke and Jacques winding up fifth and sixth, way ahead of all the other naturally aspirated runners. In fact, at the flag, they were over a lap ahead of the next naturally aspirated competitor...

From 1984 onwards, most of the British F1 constructors employed internals from the heavier-duty Hewland DGB gearbox in the transmissions used for turbo power, the general level of reliability under enormous power loadings surprising even Mike Hewland himself.

'During the turbo era, our problem was not so much a matter of increased horsepower, but the massive increase in torque which jumped from about 250 lb/ft in the heyday of the DFV to as much as 400 lb/ft with the most powerful turbos,' he reflects. 'When I think of our tiny first-gear ratios, which can be covered by the palm of your hand, and then see all the ferocious power that goes through them at the start of a Grand Prix, I sometimes wonder how anybody gets off the grid at all!'

Patrick Head is similarly impressed with the durability and staying power demonstrated by the Hewland internals. 'If you had told me that we would regularly be putting somewhere in the region of 900 bhp through gears which started out dealing with something like 300 bhp twenty years ago, then I would have been hard-pushed to believe it,' he smiles.

Tyrrell was another team which took the decision to make its own gearbox casing in 1979, especially designed to permit the coil-spring/damper units to be tucked well inboard alongside the transmission for use in its early ground-effect designs. Interestingly, the McLaren boss then, Teddy Mayer, did a deal with Tyrrell to use this casing on the McLaren M30 in 1980, the last of the team's cars to be built prior to the merger with Ron Dennis's Project 4 organisation out of which McLaren International was born.

The following year John Barnard was preoccupied designing the new carbon-fibre composite MP4/4 and, much as he would have liked to produce a totally new transmission case, continued to use the Tyrrell-derived casting on the new car. 'With all the problems involved making the new chassis, there just wasn't the time or resources available,' he explained, 'and when you start designing round such a major component as a gearbox, it is not at all easy to get a change initiated.' As a result, another deal was concluded with Tyrrell to make further modifications to the casting, and this lasted the McLaren–TAGs right through to the end of their competitive life in 1987. 'We kept nibbling away at the pattern,' Barnard remembers, 'and we stuck with the smaller FGB gear sizes, even when some of our rivals switched to the heavier-duty FGB ratios which were quite a lot bigger.'

By 1984 the McLaren team was having all its own gears manufactured in the USA by either Emco or Arrow Gears; paying very close attention to detail and fine tuning, a six-speed unit was evolved which ran with a generally high standard of reliability through to the end of the 1987 season.

The McLaren transmissions, of course, were essentially conventional in layout, with their gear packs sticking out behind the crown wheel and pinion. The team retained this configuration on the Honda turbo-engined MP4/4 introduced at the start of 1988, but the very low crankshaft position on the Honda RA168-E engine meant that it was necessary to 'step up' the drive to a level which would minimise the driveshaft angularity. This was done by means of a new three-shaft transmission developed by two of Gordon Murray's old confederates, David North and Pete Weismann. The extra shaft revolves at engine speed and produces a slight power loss as well, but its pre-season endurance runs on Weismann's California-based test bed revealed it to be extremely reliable – as was subsequently emphasised when Alain Prost won at Rio. The McLaren approach to packaging the transmission under the footbox regulations introduced for 1988 made for a slightly

The Benetton B188 features a gear cluster ahead of the rear axle-line in order to balance wheelbase requirements in the light of the 1988 technical rules requiring the driver's feet to be behind the front axle-line.

longer wheelbase than some thought ideal, contrasting with the efforts made by the Benetton and Williams teams with their new naturally aspirated B188 and FW12 respectively.

Benetton's Rory Byrne, heading a design team led by Dave Wass and Paul Crooks, faced a switch from turbo to naturally aspirated Ford–Cosworth power as well as conforming with the new chassis regulations. In order to retain a weight distribution similar to that of the highly promising B187, they positioned the gear pack between the engine and the rear axle-line, designing a totally new transmission which made use of smaller gears thanks to the lower level of torque developed by the naturally aspirated 3.5-litre engine.

Coincidentally, Wass had previously been Chief Designer for the Arrows team and had produced a similar 'inboard' gearbox for the abortive A9 in the summer of 1986. Thierry Boutsen was one of the Arrows team's drivers at the time and recalled the experiments with this new transmission as being inconclusive, 'although it was difficult to draw an accurate conclusion because the A9 was such a terrible car'. Ironically, in a vain attempt to improve its handling, the inboard transmission was shelved and the car fitted with a more conventional Hewland-based gearbox from the earlier Arrows A8. It made little difference, but once Boutsen sampled the new Benetton transmission he was immediately impressed with how slick and precise it felt.

Over at Williams, transmission engineer Enrique Scalabroni worked with Patrick Head on the development of a neat transverse gearbox, to be positioned ahead of the rear axle-line, to mate with the 3.5-litre Judd engine the team planned to use after losing Honda turbo power at the end of the previous year. Using what were basically lightweight Hewland DG gears, specially manufactured to Williams's own specifications with narrower gear teeth and thinner discs, the new unit was confirmed as 'considerably lighter' than its immediate predecessor on the 1987 FW11B–Honda. Informed sources suggest that the new Williams gearbox may weigh as much as 40 per cent less, contributing to a superbly integrated and compact overall package with which to take on the turbos in their last season.

As far as future F1 transmission development is concerned, it is not merely in the area of component variety that progress is likely to be made over the next few years. The possibility of a new generation of V12 3.5-litre Grand Prix engines will probably give rise to a fresh crop of transverse gearbox layouts, similar to the Williams in concept. Lamborghini's new V12, currently being developed for Chrysler, may well be mated to a new transverse gearbox and, since March Racing is one of the teams which will test the Italian V12 later in 1988, there is considerable speculation as to whether the link between the two companies will produce a new partnership in transmission development. March have already spent a great deal of engineering effort developing their own Indy car transmissions in addition to F1 gearboxes using internals from Staffs Silent Gears. There is certainly potential for harnessing the specialist engineering skills of the Italian company to the racing expertise of the March group, both in F1 and production racing car applications.

Ferrari, of course, are never far behind when it comes to gearbox development. At the time of writing, the new John Barnard-designed naturally aspirated 3.5-litre V12-engined F188 is nearing completion at Maranello. From the outset it will be equipped with an electrically controlled, hydraulically actuated press-button clutch mechanism. The system has been tried out in private at the team's Fiorano test track, fitted to one of the updated F187 turbo V6s which Gerhard Berger and Michele Alboreto were scheduled to drive throughout the 1988 season. It promises to offer a worthwhile technical edge and may set a trend soon to be followed by Ferrari's rivals.

Chapter 4

The light at the end of the tunnel

Until the early 1970s it was not uncommon to see Grand Prix cars testing with tufts of string stuck, apparently haphazardly, all over their bodywork. This was a crude and often ineffective means of gaining knowledge about the airflow over the car, although today's aerodynamicists tend to shudder when they recall these unrefined experiments. As an aside, it is perhaps ironic that the only F1 car the writer actually saw so equipped was one of Frank Williams's machines, during the summer of 1972. A few years later, once established as one of the top teams, Williams Grand Prix Engineering became the first F1 organisation to install its own wind-tunnel facility. A far cry from those early, primitive experiments…

Aerodynamics has always been crucially important to the performance of any racing car, although it is only over the past couple of decades that there has been universal appreciation of just how essential an element it is. Think back three decades to the all-enveloping bodywork of the World Constructors' Championship-winning Vanwalls, pencilled by Frank Costin. He paid enormous attention to detail, including making the under-car profile as smooth and uncluttered as possible. Bearing that in mind it seems inconceivable, knowing what we know now, that anybody could have expected the 1966-67 Cooper–Maserati to have been anything but a ponderous old tug. Heavy, ungainly and aerodynamically lacking, it was designed with the 'engine power is all' philosophy which also characterised Ferrari's and Honda's contemporary efforts. Yet, only a year later, the benefits of an aerodynamically sound, nimble chassis were displayed to good effect when Lotus produced the 49. It set a new dimension in 3-litre GP car performance, a not altogether surprising development when one recalls it had all these plus-points and the strongest engine in the business too.

However, the basic profile of the car proved to be only one element of the multi-faceted aerodynamic package. In 1968 Formula 1 cars suddenly began sprouting aerofoils to produce additional downforce, a move which prompted a sudden increase in the amount of attention paid to aerodynamic development. Jim Hall's Chaparral sports car, with its high rear wing mounted on struts above the rear wheels, first drew everybody's attention, and although it was not until Chris Amon's Ferrari 312 appeared in the 1968 Belgian Grand Prix at Spa that wings first broke into the Grand Prix game, Jim Clark's mechanics had cobbled together a makeshift aerofoil during the previous winter's Tasman series and briefly tried it on the Scot's Lotus 49T

during practice for one of the races 'down under'.

This development was followed by a rash of high wings, some mounted on bodywork, others on the top of suspension uprights, but the wind was taken out of everybody's sails when Jochen Rindt was involved in a massive accident during the 1969 Spanish Grand Prix at Barcelona and the sport's governing body (then the CSI) stepped in and banned them almost overnight. But there is, of course, no way in which technology can be 'uninvented' and, sure enough, wings have stayed as a permanent fitment on racing cars ever since, albeit more firmly (in most cases) secured to the cars.

Wings used on modern racing cars are very similar in profile to those used in aircraft design, with the one major difference that they are mounted upside down so as to develop downforce rather than generate lift. A low-pressure area is formed when air is accelerated, so with the longer side of the wing section facing downwards, the air flowing across it has to travel further and, as a consequence, speeds up. The velocity energy of air is related to its momentum and, since air has constant potential energy, as it speeds up, the pressure drops to maintain that constant energy. The resultant low-pressure area beneath the upturned wing produces downforce, sucking the wing towards the road and therefore pressing down on the suspension/bodywork, depending on where the mounting is fitted.

This raises another dimension when it comes to the complex business of setting up a contemporary Grand Prix car for a specific circuit. How much of the downforce in the corners does one trade in exchange for lack of drag and consequently improved straightline speed? This is where a sensitive driver and an experienced race engineer can collaborate to gain a worthwhile performance advantage over their rivals.

Throughout the early 1970s, the tempo of aerodynamic development really began to speed up. Bit by bit, the significance of harnessing the airflow both over and under the car was increasingly appreciated, but much of the development was relatively unscientific by the high-tech standards that have become the norm in the 1980s. A mixture of intuition, feel and previous experience, plus the odd bit of wind-tunnel work, represented the limit of aerodynamic investigation for many teams.

Frank Dernie, the Williams team's highly respected aerodynamicist, feels that some people within the sport still take a rather simplistic view of aerodynamics. 'To put it in perspective, there is still an old guard that believes that wings should be banned – and by banning wings you will be, in effect, banning aerodynamics. They don't understand that the aerodynamic package of a car doesn't just involve how the air flows over its wings; it's a question of considering the entire airflow, both over and under the car,' he explains.

Clearly, good aerodynamics on their own will not make a car competitive if, for example, it is unnecessarily overweight or has a significantly less powerful engine than its rivals. Different designers apply differing technical priorities to their designs. Some put the emphasis on torsional stiffness, some on suspension geometry, some on aerodynamics – but that is not to say that any element is ignored. It is a question of striking the right compromise, and then ensuring it works properly out on the circuit.

Trading straightline speed for downforce is the perpetual equation tackled by F1 designers and one of the first to stumble on the benefits of low-pressure areas beneath the cars was Brabham's Gordon Murray, way back in 1974. At that time Gordon's second complete Brabham design, the triangular monocoque BT44, was impressing many rival teams with its seemingly exceptional straightline speed and competitive overall lap times. True, it was a compact design with a relatively narrow track while the triangular monocoque, in Murray's estimation, was moving like an air dam and excluding a lot of air from beneath the car. As he says: 'I reckoned that the car never bottomed out in the centre of the monocoque's underside, so we tried putting a forward-facing V-shaped skirt beneath the car in an attempt to exclude even more air. Although I didn't appreciate all the subtleties at the time, what we were doing was to produce an area of low pressure under the car which meant that we could start backing off the conventional wing angle and run slightly quicker in a straight line. I estimated those V-shaped skirts were giving us around 150 pounds of additional downforce.'

For Brabham, the game was finally up at the Österreichring when McLaren Chief Mechanic Alistair Caldwell got a close look at those plastic skirts beneath the Brabham, when the car was up on jacks in the pit lane. He reported back to his team, they twigged what was going on and, within a race or two, the McLaren M23s appeared with fixed plastic skirts, angled slightly outwards at the lower edge, around the lower perimeter of the monocoque. Ground effect was on its way, albeit in a pretty basic form.

By the mid-1970s, the use of wind tunnels to check and analyse aerodynamic performance was becoming a regular feature of Grand Prix car development. The Motor Industry Research Association (MIRA) had a full-scale tunnel available, but most of the significant racing car development during that decade was probably produced by quarter-scale model tunnels, with a rolling road, such as the Imperial College tunnel in London and the similar facility at Southampton University. Williams now has one, in-house, at Didcot. Benetton has exclusive use of the tunnel at Shrivenham's Royal Military Laboratory, McLaren test at the National Marine Laboratories at Teddington and Lotus, most recently, at the Comtec tunnel at Brackley, near Silverstone, which is operated by one of March boss Robin Herd's companies.

Frank Dernie gives credit to Tony Southgate and the Shadow team as being one of the first F1 outfits to obtain valid results from a quarter-scale wind tunnel using a rolling road. 'Working at Imperial College with John Harvey and Peter Bearman, they made a good deal of progress with their DN8 design and then, of course, Peter Wright came along and really began to get stuck into the business of ground effect.'

As to whether a full-scale wind tunnel is a more accurate proposition than one which uses scale models, Dernie finds it difficult to reach a conclusion. 'I frankly believe it is impossible to reach an accurate conclusion on that point,' he says, 'because nobody has the data to prove the point one way or another. Suffice to say, I have indications that a full-size wind tunnel does not always produce the same sort of results I believe we get with the car when it is out on the circuit. But it is difficult to correlate the two situations. Take, as an individual example, a test outing at the Österreichring in 1987. Our car was accelerating from 100 to 150 mph in about three seconds and it is enormously difficult to duplicate this sort of situation, accurately, in a wind tunnel.'

However, the awareness that under-car airflow was something that, sometime, somehow, could be effectively harnessed to produce downforce was a fact which had been through several designers' minds over the years. Peter Wright tinkered with a very crude wing car with aerodynamic side pods during his time at BRM, while Robin Herd's March 701 raced with such pods throughout 1970. They were developed again by Wright who, by then, had quit BRM and moved on to work for the Huntingdon-based firm Specialised Mouldings, the plastic moulding company who were one of the first within the motor racing industry to invest in a wind tunnel. Interestingly, it was later sold to the Williams team!

Wright admits to this day that he was 'not proud' of the 701 side pods but, over the next few years, he gained an enormous amount of additional knowledge about aerodynamics with work on powerboat hulls for Johnson-Evinrude. Then came the crucial move. He was approached to work for Technocraft, a company within Group Lotus which was experimenting in new injection-moulding techniques. Then, soon after Tony Rudd was brought in to oversee the Ketteringham Hall R & D programme for Team Lotus, Wright was called in on the aerodynamic side.

Inspired by Colin Chapman's 'amazing knack for feeling whether an idea was fundamentally right or wrong', Peter soon became enthusiastically immersed in the long-term plans to revive Lotus's F1 fortunes. 'With our initial work on ground effect, Colin was convinced that he could get something for nothing in terms of enhanced car performance – in other words, tremendous downforce without the penalty being exacted in reduced straightline speed. He pursued the whole thing with enormous vigour,' Wright recalls.

It was while working with models of the still-secret Lotus 78 in the Imperial College wind tunnel that Wright, almost accidentally, stumbled across possibly the most significant discovery of all, something which would, as things turned out, have enormous long-term significance for F1 racing car development over the following five years. During tests to finalise the car's basic layout, including assessing whether the water radiators could be buried within the leading edges of the side pods and still cool successfully (they could), Wright began getting non-repeatable results with the wind-tunnel model.

'On close inspection, I found that the side pods on the model were sagging and, as the pods went down, so the downforce increased. We decided that this ought to be explored further and quickly cut up some side panels out of cardboard which extended right down to the ground. The downforce immediately doubled! It was at this point that we began to appreciate just how important the integration of a skirt design into the overall concept would be. We were all very concerned at Lotus that skirts might not be deemed within the regulations, so we examined the whole matter very carefully and the 78 first raced with brushes bridging the gap between the underside of the pods and the ground,' he explains.

The advent of this first ground-effect Lotus concentrated rival designers' minds wonderfully well. But although the 78 acted as a technical catalyst within F1, it also threw a lot of people who were still doggedly concentrating on other design elements. Few of Chapman's rivals believed that the type 78 really developed such massive amounts of aerodynamic downforce, and Lotus proved very clever at putting people off the scent. Low-percentage slip differentials and a preferential fuel drainage system, allied to Mario Andretti's knowledge of such Indy car techniques as corner-weighting (diagonal stiffness adjusted in the spring platforms) helped create the illusion that the car's performance was just a question of good balance and sensitive driving. True, good weight distribution was one of the 78's major plus-points, but it was by no means the key to its superior track performance.

All Chapman had done was to harness the low-pressure area that everybody knew existed beneath conventional aerofoils. Controlling that 'centre of pressure' – the point at which the vertical downforce generated by the side pods was at its maximum – thereafter became the most crucial element in the design of ground-effect racing cars. Endless hours of wind-tunnel time were expended to evolve the optimum side-pod profile for specific cars.

The object of the exercise was to produce an airflow which exited the diffuser section beneath the car at driving speed, or just above it. In order to bring about the requisite downforce, the air had to be drawn into the diffuser at three times exit speed, producing the maximum downforce at the point where the space between the underside of the car and the track surface is at its narrowest. However, in those pioneering days of ground effect, a lot of people thought that the expansion of the air under the car was creating a low-pressure area towards the rear of the chassis.

The effect in terms of downforce loadings on the car was quite remarkable. At around 60 mph the car would generate around 550 lb of downforce, but that would leap to somewhere in the region of 5000 lb at 180 mph. In other words, the all-up weight of a stationary car would be multiplied by a factor of four when the car was running at high speed, squeezing every ounce of potential from its ground-effect aerodynamics.

Of course, whether a designer could produce a ground-effect car depended, to a large extent, on what basic mechanical package he had to start with. Building one's car round the compact Ford–Cosworth DFV 3-litre V8, with its narrow bottom end, made it a fairly straightforward business to outline a basic ground-effect concept with wide venturis on either side of the car. However, this was a luxury which Brabham designer Gordon Murray, for one, did not enjoy in 1978. By a convoluted route, therefore, he conceived one of the most novel and outrageous high downforce racing cars of all time – the Brabham BT46B, known to all and sundry as 'the fan car'.

Brabham had initially planned a radically new car to carry the powerful flat-12 Alfa Romeo engine in 1978, using a complicated system of surface cooling by means of heat exchangers mounted on the outer surface of the distinctive pyramidal monocoque. Murray's wind-tunnel work convinced him that the car would cool sufficiently well with this system but, in the event, the BT46 overheated after only a couple of laps round Donington Park and Silverstone in the depths of winter. If it did that, it was clearly not going to be much use in the heat of Buenos Aires…

Gordon therefore had to compromise the BT46's aerodynamics by slinging nose-mounted radiators on the cars for the first half of the year, but regarded this as a short-term solution. By now Colin Chapman had come up with the ultra-competitive Lotus 79, a refinement of the ground-effect type 78. The underwing sections on the first Lotus wing car had been concentrated well forward, giving the front end an enormous amount of 'bite'

Two views of the Williams wind-tunnel facility which was originally purchased from Specialised Mouldings and developed by the team's talented aerodynamicist, Frank Dernie.

78

when it came to turn-in which the rear end never really matched up to. Thus, in order to produce more downforce at the rear, the 78s tended to run rather more in the way of conventional downforce from their rear wings than had originally been intended. That's why they were slow on the straights. But more intensive wind-tunnel work resulted in the type 79's smoother, longer, more progressive underbody profile which continued right to the rear of the car, the airflow through which was not cluttered and confused by suspension members and exhaust pipes. If the 78 had pointed the way, the 79 restated the parameters of Grand Prix car performance. Nobody could ignore it – or get on terms with it.

Gordon Murray and his assistant, David North, sat down and read through the technical regulations very carefully indeed, particularly bearing in mind the definitions of aerodynamic devices which, at the time, were described as 'any part of the car whose *primary function* is to influence aerodynamic performance'. Under Article 3, item 7, the rules stated: 'Aerodynamic devices must comply with the rules relating to coachwork and must be firmly fixed while the car is in motion. It is permissible to bridge the gap between the coachwork and the ground by means of flexible structures subject to the coachwork regulations.' That latter provision took care of skirts. But Murray and North kept the first part of the provision in their mind while they evolved their striking new secret weapon.

For the first couple of races of the 1978 season, in South America, Brabham had fielded uprated versions of the previous season's cars while

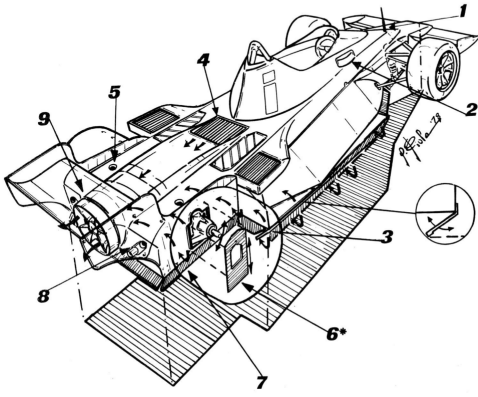

The Brabham BT46 'fan car' used a vertically mounted fan (9) on the rear of the car, ostensibly to suck hot air from the water radiator (4) mounted on top of the flat-12 engine. However, it also enabled a low-pressure area to be created beneath the skirted underbody perimeter, thereby producing downforce. A pitot head (1) was mounted on the nose of the car, the airspeed indicator for the driver being mounted in a 'bubble' on the inner wall of the cockpit (2). Sealing the skirt, particularly at points 3, 6 and 7, was crucial to the operational success of the concept.

*The late Ronnie Peterson rounds Druids
hairpin at Brands Hatch during the 1978
British Grand Prix at the wheel of Colin
Chapman's Lotus 79, the most influential
design of the 'first generation' of ground-
effect cars.*

Renault pioneered contemporary F1 turbo technology, the French team making its debut at the 1977 British Grand Prix. By the time this shot of Jean-Pierre Jabouille was taken at Silverstone two years later, the state-owned industrial giant had already scored its first Grand Prix win with the neat ground-effect RS11 chassis.

*Carlos Reutemann's fixed-skirt Williams
FW07C gets briefly airborne over a brow at
Long Beach, 1981. In response to the revised
regulations introduced that year, designers
strove to maintain a constant ride height,
resulting in ultra-stiff suspension set-ups
which made the cars difficult to control and
tiring to drive.*

*Keke Rosberg heading for second place at the
Österreichring in 1982 at the wheel of the
Williams FW08, essentially a 'cleaned up'
derivative of the FW07 series. Rosberg became
World Champion at the wheel of this car.*

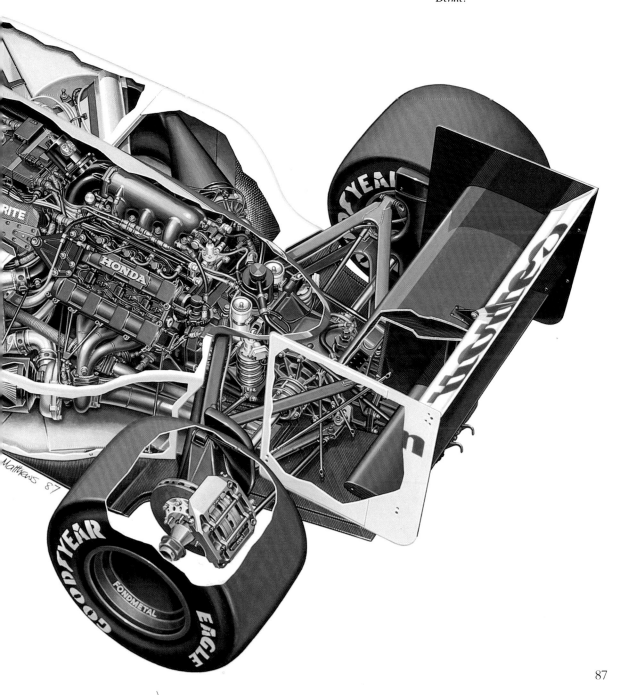

The World Champion car of 1987, the Canon Williams–Honda FW11B won nine races in the hands of Nigel Mansell (six) and Nelson Piquet (three). An evolutionary version of the previous season's FW11, its high standards of build quality and detail finish were a credit to the efforts of the Williams team, reflecting Patrick Head's knowledge of constructional techniques and a highly developed aerodynamic profile evolved in Williams's own wind tunnel by Frank Dernie.

Gordon Murray's last design for the Brabham team was the striking yet over-complex 'low-line' BT55. Among its more successful rivals in 1986 were the John Barnard-designed McLaren–TAG MP4/2C (inset, centre) *and the Harvey Postlethwaite-designed Ferrari F186* (inset, right).

*Benetton testing their B187's profile in the
Shrivenham wind tunnel, early 1987.*

Right: **McLaren's MP4/4** *– the car of 1988. In
accounting for the team's remarkable
success, most commentators have pointed to
the power and economy of the Honda engine,
while acknowledging the skills of drivers
Prost and Senna. But, beneath the skin, the
black carbon-fibre chassis has performed a
crucial, if often overlooked, role.*

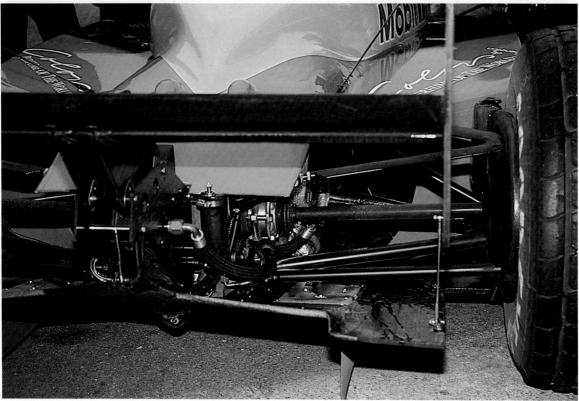

Top left: **The Williams reactive suspension
employed on the FW12 operates in
conjunction with double wishbones and
pushrods. The 'stepped' rear diffuser panel
treatment on Benetton's B188 is notably neat**
(below left).

The uncluttered installation of the
Ford–Cosworth DFR in the rear of the
1988 Benetton.

The Benetton B188 features an inboard gear cluster, outboard brakes and exhaust exits through the diffuser panel.

work on fixing nose radiators to the BT46s continued back at base. These BT45Cs had been fitted with a small electric fan, atop the flat-12 engine and just below the horizontally mounted oil coolers, the intention being to help the airflow through those coolers. What Murray now planned followed on, obliquely, from that line of thinking.

After briefly toying with the concept of a conventional water radiator mounted on top of the engine, Murray finalized a configuration which employed a large water radiator mounted horizontally above the flat-12, the whole engine/gearbox assembly sealed off from the outside air by means of flexible skirts and a large, gearbox-driven fan to suck out all the air from beneath the engine/gearbox bay. It took a considerable amount of experimentation with skirts, fan speeds and radiator sizes to arrive at the optimum set-up, most of this work being carried out at Alfa Romeo's Balocco test track.

Probably the single most challenging aspect of the whole concept was getting the gearbox drive working correctly. Concern that the adoption of a direct-drive system from the bottom shaft of the gearbox would put enormous strain on the gearchange, due to the fact that the gear shaft would continue revolving because of the fan's inertia when the drive engaged the clutch, proved happily unfounded. A sprag clutch was fitted at the end of the bottom shaft so that the fan would de-couple when the driver depressed the clutch. However, this seized solid on its first outing and the gearchange mechanism worked fine, so Murray concluded that he had over-engineered the whole system. The cars therefore went to their first race in Sweden, the only one they would contest, with a direct-drive system.

Murray contended that the fan car was within the spirit and letter of the regulations, pointing out that a CSI technical commission had examined it and broadly agreed with his assessment that the fan was employed about 70 per cent for cooling and 30 per cent to generate downforce. But that did not prevent Lotus and Tyrrell both protesting after Niki Lauda had driven the fan car to a commanding victory in the Swedish Grand Prix, and it was eventually legislated out of the business. Murray, to this day, believes that banning it was really unnecessary. 'It was a short-term expedient. I don't believe that such a system would ever have developed the sort of downforce that we were destined to see during the 1979 and '80 Grand Prix seasons, for example.'

Meanwhile, to the uninitiated outside observer, there seemed little reason to suppose that the Lotus 79 would fail to sustain its edge in 1979, such was the margin of performance by which it had outstripped the opposition in 1978. It didn't work out that way, although it took most teams an amazingly long time to pick up the threads of ground effect. Chapman forged on with a totally new ground-effect car which, on paper at least, with its full-length skirts and small aerofoils, looked like being another winner.

'However, by then we were moving into an area of totally new problems,' explains Peter Wright, 'because we found ourselves grappling with too much downforce and simply did not know how to handle it.' The idea was to produce longer, lower-drag underwing profiles which would virtually dispense with the need for conventional wings and nose fins, thereby further reducing the car's overall drag at no cost in terms of lost downforce. That was the thinking, at any rate, behind the Lotus 80.

Wind-tunnel testing has been a vital facet of F1 car development over recent years. Here a quarter-scale model of the 1981 Ligier JS17 undergoes adjustments prior to a series of tests.

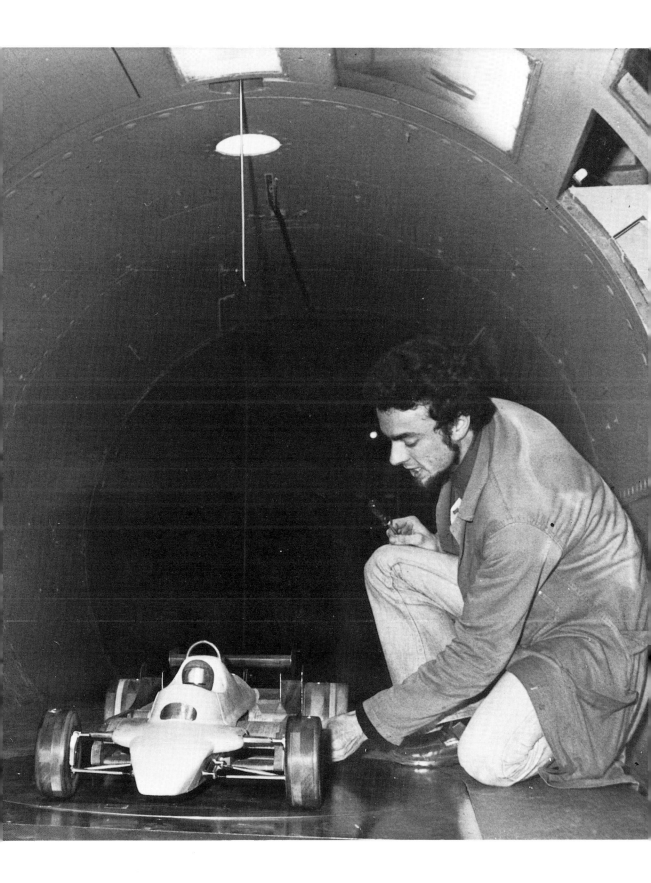

Alfa Romeo built a new V12 engine specifically so that Gordon Murray could maximise the ground-effect potential of the 1979 Brabham BT48, seen here in its striking original configuration with low rear wing.

Coincidentally, over at Brabham, Gordon Murray had been thinking along the same lines, largely through force of circumstance. It was clear that there was no way in which he could produce a vaguely competitive ground-effect package if the team continued with the flat-12 Alfa engine, so Autodelta pulled out all the stops to produce a brand new V12 engine, specifically for incorporation into a ground-effect design, within a matter of months. The chassis Gordon built to accept this engine was the striking BT48, its rear wing little more than a full-width flap along the tail end of the engine cover – between small end plates – and with not a nose wing to be seen.

Unfortunately, the BT48 suffered from what was to become a dreaded affliction during the ground-effect era – 'porpoising'. This amounted to an uncontrollable fore/aft pitching movement. Once the seal between the crucial aerodynamic side skirts and the track surface was broken, ambient-pressure air leaked into the underwing area, with the result that the car bounced free of the ground as it stopped being sucked down onto the track.

Such problems taught all designers that sliding skirts must be allowed to move as freely as possible within their runners. The moment a skirt stuck up, for any reason, the car lost all its downforce and rode up on its suspension; that in turn released the skirts, they fell back into contact with the track and the downforce was restored. Then the skirts rode up over the next bump and the whole cycle began again. It should also be remembered that the proximity to the ground of a certain side-pod profile could have a profound influence on its effectiveness. One section could be working perfectly, but might then 'stall' if it was lowered even as little as an inch closer to the ground. It stopped producing downforce, so the suspension caused the car to rise up again, the flow re-attached and the ground effect was restored.

One of the crucial requirements for a ground-effect car was to have side pods which would not in themselves deflect under aerodynamic loadings. That was one area in which the Williams FW07 set fresh standards, there being some evidence that the Lotus 78 side pods, for example, had not been quite as rigid as would have been ideal. If the side pods were not adequately supported, then there was the ever-present problem of the wing profile changing under load, introducing more quirks to the car's track performance.

Team Lotus being suddenly toppled from its pre-eminent position at the pinnacle of F1 technical achievement in 1979 prompted Chapman's R & D department at Ketteringham Hall to take steps towards redressing the situation. The way in which aerodynamic loadings had dramatically increased with the second generation of ground-effect machines preoccupied their thoughts and they turned to examining ways in which the aerodynamic forces could be isolated from the chassis itself.

The result of Chapman's deliberations with Peter Wright turned out to be the remarkable twin-chassis Lotus 86, a design which was conceived in conformity with the current regulations then permitting the use of aerodynamic side skirts. However, the era of sliding-skirt cars had put a premium on clever chassis technology and innovative engineering, factors which favoured the predominantly British-based specialist constructors rather than the 'grandees' headed by Ferrari and Renault. Renault, with its turbocharged engines, had prodigious power available to pull large conventional aerofoils, but they just did not have the chassis technology on a par with Williams, for example. Ferrari, who had squeezed through 1979 by the skin of their technical teeth, using a combination of excellent Michelin rubber, a responsive and punchy flat-12 engine and the best lash-up compromise of a ground-effect chassis they could assemble within the dimensional constraints of a flat-12 engine, then collapsed into disarray with the hopeless 312T5 of 1980.

Jody Scheckter and Gilles Villeneuve lent their weight to the outcry, in part orchestrated by Renault, that sliding-skirt ground-effect cars were unsafe. Taking an uncharitable point of view, bearing in mind that the T5's sliding-skirt system was very poor, they may have been right, at least as far as their cars were concerned. But the way in which lap speeds increased, and cornering speeds increased, was sufficient to sound the alarm bells within the corridors of the sport's governing body in Paris. FISA banned sliding skirts and enforced a 6 cm ground-clearance rule for the 1981 season, despite the fact that most team designers and engineers knew full well that such a system would be absolutely impossible to police.

Fixed-length skirts were permitted, along with sculptured underbody profiles, so the moment any engineer came up with a system of lowering the suspension when the car was on the move, ground effect still survived. With a brand of technical ingenuity similar to that which he had employed to develop the fan car, Gordon Murray, again with David North's assistance, came up with a mechanism which was to cause a storm of protest and indignation on the part of the Brabham team's rivals.

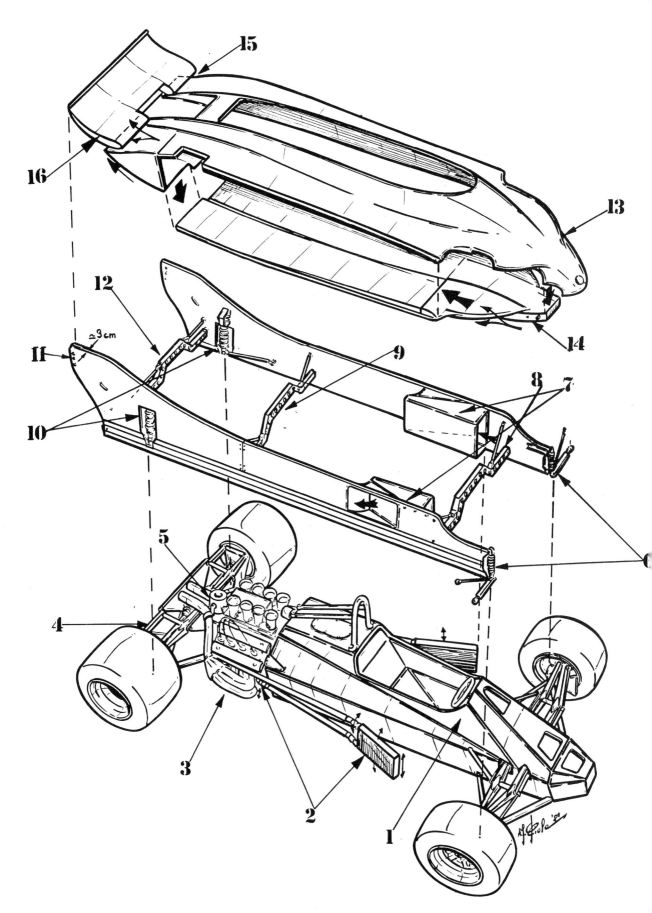

The Lotus 'twin chassis' concept involved a basic monocoque/suspension/engine assembly onto which a separately suspended structure was mounted by three cross-beams (8, 9 and 12). The water radiators were also attached to this second sprung structure which insulated the aerodynamic loadings through small coil-springs front and rear (6 and 10). The basic chassis used Chapman's carbon-fibre/Kevlar construction, being beaten by the McLaren MP4 by the margin of a few days in the race to be the first F1 design employing carbon fibre to be unveiled.

This employed a system of soft air springs which the aerodynamic load compressed as the speed built up, dropping the then-current BT49C down into a ground-effect stance and allowing the team to obtain an appreciable performance advantage. As the car slowed, it would rise on its springs to conform with the 6 cm ground-clearance rule. The efficiency of the system was underlined when not only did Nelson Piquet run away with the Argentine Grand Prix at Buenos Aires, but his journeyman number two, Hector Rebaque, surged imperiously past Carlos Reutemann's Williams to take second place before retiring with a broken rotor arm.

In Frank Williams's view, at the time, it mattered not that the Brabhams were running a novel hydro-pneumatic suspension system, but that the cars were not running the fixed skirts which, in his view, the new regulations required. Murray countered by insisting that the cars were legal according to the new rules, and FISA's wonderful step in the interests of racing safety showed every sign of becoming very badly unstuck. Eventually, FISA issued one of its famous 'rule clarifications', a ploy frequently utilised to change regulations at a stroke without worrying too much about any long-term stability clauses – and it was decided that it would only be permissible to run skirts no more than 3 cm deep and with a uniform thickness of between 5 cm and 6 cm.

In Argentina, the Brabhams had run with 3 cm fixed skirts fitted to the BT49Cs, with a thicker block on the bottom edge for an additional degree of abrade resistance. FISA's 'new rule' simply intensified debate as to how rigid was rigid. At Imola, venue for the San Marino Grand Prix, the Brabham team found its rivals effectively 'ganging up' against Murray's interpretation of the rules with the result that official scrutineers arrived and said 'those skirts are too flexible' after making only the most cursory examination. Murray, exasperated, replied: 'OK, you go and get us some material *you* think conforms with the regulations and we'll make a set of skirts out of it.' The officials obliged, Brabham made up the new skirts – and Piquet won the race. 'I enjoyed that!' grinned Gordon afterwards...

Meanwhile, Chapman's R & D team at Ketteringham Hall came up with Lotus's way of tackling what had now evolved into a totally stupid set of technical regulations. Skirted Grand Prix cars may well have thrown the technical initiative to the innovative British constructors but, properly engineered, they at least had predictable handling characteristics and their suspensions, though regarded as stiff by the standards of their time, were not in the same league as the rock-hard breed of F1 machines which were spawned by the fixed-skirt rules. FISA may have known what it was seeking to achieve, but the route by which it set out to reduce cornering speeds was strewn with technical problems.

Lotus's answer was the twin-chassis type 86, originally tested at the end of 1980 during the last season of the sliding-skirt regulations. Wind-tunnel testing had convinced Chapman's team that, instead of having separate sliding skirts moving up and down relative to the bodywork, it would be better to spring-mount the body structure atop the wheel uprights, thereby transmitting the aerodynamic loadings directly to the suspension and tyres, while also incorporating a conventionally sprung chassis riding free within the movable aerodynamic body. This brilliant concept killed two birds with one stone, stabilising the under-car aerodynamics while at the same time

Aerodynamic 'winglets', located ahead of the rear axle-line and therefore legal, were used by many teams in 1983 to retrieve lost ground-effect downforce. These examples adorn a Brabham BT53 *(top)* and a McLaren MP4/1C. Such aerodynamic appendages were forbidden from the start of 1985 in an attempt to check the turbo generation's ever-increasing lap speeds.

precluding the driver from the physical battering which was now an inevitable byproduct of ultra-stiff suspension.

This was a fundamentally intelligent and aerodynamically sound means of blending together the requirements of consistent and predictable performance with driver comfort and security, but FISA got wind of what Chapman was up to and issued yet another of its 'rule clarifications' to Article 3, clause 7: 'Any specific part of the car influencing its aerodynamic performance – must comply with the rules relating to bodywork; must be rigidly secured to the entirely sprung part of the car (rigidly means not having any degree of freedom); and must remain immobile in relation to the sprung part of the car.'

The Lotus boss remained absolutely convinced that the sport's governing body had no business or power interfering with the clause imposing rule stability for two years – a clause which FISA itself had only just had a major hand in enacting – and pressed on with the construction of a fixed-skirt version of the 86, now based round a carbon/Kevlar monocoque rather than the 86's aluminium honeycomb chassis. He presented it just before the start of the season.

The new type 88 would, in Chapman's view, solve the problem of pitch-sensitivity which had dogged his ground-effect efforts with the type 80 two years earlier. Resisting such pitch had meant stiffening springs to the point where half the suspension movement was coming from deflection within the rocker arms, a test of the car's structure which was as unnecessary as it was unsatisfactory, not to mention the pounding received by the luckless driver. Anyway, to cut a long story short, a succession of protests and unfavourable edicts from FISA spelt the downfall of the 'twin-chassis' Lotus before it was ever permitted to take part in a race. Technical ingenuity had been stifled simply because the rest of the herd was ag'in it.

Throughout 1981 and into 1982 spring rates gradually climbed to beyond the 3000-lb mark as designers fought to control the behaviour of their fixed skirts, these efforts quickly producing a breed of 200 mph go-karts from which bruised and battered drivers emerged periodically to recount horrific tales of close shaves which their difficult-to-control cars were unable to avoid. Ironically, skirt technology developed into a black art all of its own, wind-tunnel tests and on-track experimentation being relied upon to produce the most ideal set-up for any particular day.

Frank Dernie: 'When we were running the Williams FW08 in 1982, the degree of flexibility of the material used to make its fixed skirts was the most crucial key to its performance. We had four or five different skirt thicknesses, all related to the amount of wing we might be running in a given place in addition to driver input on the day. Not only that, but they were stiffer towards the front end of the skirt, where the pressure under the side pod was at its lowest, gradually becoming less stiff towards the rear, where the pressure was not so low and, consequently, the loadings not so high. It was simply a question of running the stiffest skirts you could get away with without causing the car to start porpoising.

'These skirts were also incredibly sensitive to the ambient temperature. As an example, the 1982 Canadian Grand Prix at Montreal was delayed by Riccardo Paletti's tragic fatal startline accident, by which time the temperature had dropped significantly and we found that the skirts on Keke's car

were effectively one grade too stiff. He reported that the car was almost undrivable for much of the race.'

These flexi-skirt ground-effect cars were undoubtedly some of the most difficult machines to drive to the outer limit of their potential. Any driver who said that sliding-skirt ground-effect cars were 'too easy' to drive was almost certainly not extracting the full potential from his chassis.

Aside from major aerodynamic considerations, there were also subtle changes being made, the reasons behind which were not always totally obvious at the time. For example, the trend away from rocker-arm suspension systems to pullrod arrangements did not just reflect a belief that the changes produced fundamentally better suspension systems. In 1982, the Williams FW08 supplanted the successful FW07 range, but in many ways it would have probably been as accurate to describe the new car as the FW07 'E', so evolutionary was its concept. Its side pods were exactly the same, but Frank Dernie's tests had revealed that the front suspension rocker arms and rocker fairings were generating an unwanted degree of uplift, so these aerodynamic considerations were totally behind the switch to pullrod suspension on the new car. 'At the time, people were saying that pullrod suspension is better,' said Dernie, 'but the fact is that it's really no better at all. We made the change purely because of aerodynamic considerations.'

A succession of serious accidents in 1982, notably the one which killed Ferrari's Gilles Villeneuve during practice for the Belgian Grand Prix at Zolder, followed by an equally horrifying shunt at Hockenheim later that same summer which ended the racing career of Didier Pironi, focused FISA's collective mind on the monster they had unwittingly created. Having taken the decision to ban sliding skirts, it was now decided that sculptured underbody panels would have to go: as from 1 January 1983, flat-bottom regulations would be enforced between the trailing edge of the front wheels and the leading edge of the rear.

At a stroke, F1 chassis designers lost about 60 per cent of the total downforce available to them, so the next few years were spent evolving means whereby as much of that lost downforce could be clawed back as efficiently as possible – to a large extent by using much bigger conventional aerofoils. Of course, at about this time F1 was on the verge of developing its second generation of turbocharged 1½-litre engines, with a consequent significant increase in power. This in turn allowed much bigger conventional wings to be employed, now that there was power aplenty to drag them through the air.

Frank Dernie: 'We were now looking at a totally different animal and, suddenly, long side pods tended to produce lift, so the ideal was to keep them short, although we did an enormous amount of experimentation in the wind tunnel to come up with the optimum solution. I tried a big front-wing arrangement, sweeping right back through the front suspension assembly, and tried to complement it with a similar wing-type arrangement extending through the rear suspension which, in turn, also incorporated the radiators. But we just couldn't get it to balance; there didn't seem any way we could get a worthwhile amount of downforce on the rear of the car and we eventually gave up on this configuration after half a dozen or so tries.'

Over at Brabham, Gordon Murray had come to similar conclusions about side pods. 'We were obviously looking at major problems with traction in

the small amount of wind-tunnel time available to us, but the work we did manage to do confirmed the view that the smaller side pod we could use the better.' By the time the flat-bottom rule was instigated, Murray had completed a fixed-skirt ground-effect version of the BT50–BMW, purpose-built with a small fuel tank to take fuller advantage of the pit-stop technique which the team had reintroduced the previous summer. Now Gordon had to scrap the whole project and start again from scratch, he and his design team working non-stop for three months to ready the BT52 for its race debut at Rio, in the first race of 1983. This design and constructional marathon was duly rewarded when Nelson Piquet raced to a first-time-out victory, although Keke Rosberg's naturally aspirated Williams FW08C started from pole position.

A similar sense of urgency gripped the Toleman (now Benetton) equipe, which had proudly shown off its new ground-effect TG183–Hart turbo at the end of the 1982 season, racing it in the last few Grands Prix of the year. Rory Byrne and his design team were convinced that they had produced a reasonable chassis to replace the unloved TG181 'Flying Pig' which they had used for their graduation into F1 at the beginning of the previous season. Opting for a full-width nose section into which the water radiators were packaged, Byrne derived additional rear downforce by placing an aerofoil ahead of the rear-wheel centreline, at which point it could take advantage of the maximum width regulations, and followed that with a conventional rear wing, mounted slightly lower behind it.

Admits Team Engineer Pat Symonds, 'That nose radiator set-up on the TG183B made it enormously pitch-sensitive; the front of the car would go down, developing enormous downforce which would load up the steering quite dramatically. Then it would come up under acceleration, some of the downforce would be lost, and the steering would go light again. In that respect it was a very difficult car to set up for any specific circuit. Sometimes we would get everything working pretty well and it would go superbly, but on other occasions we couldn't make it handle anywhere near so nicely.'

During the ground-effect era some cars had managed on occasion to run without nose wings, the Brabham BT48–Alfa being the first to do so, but there was no question of dispensing with these appendages once the flat-bottom rule was enforced. Every effort was made to exploit the maximum aerofoil dimensions to the full, additional 'winglets' being added to the leading edge of the main rear wing end plate by many teams, bringing out the effective wing width to the outer edges of the bodywork, and thus arriving at the same end result as the Toleman TG183B but by a slightly different route.

The uninitiated might jump to the conclusion that getting downforce to the rear of the car is not a difficult problem, the engine and gearbox ensuring that the rearward weight bias helped matters. But aerodynamicists will quickly disabuse you of this notion. The fact of the matter is that the front wings use so much of the air that there is precious little energy left for the rear wing.

Of course, the optimum function of a wing is achieved when the airflow to and from it – the afflux and tailflow – is not interrupted. Clearly, the rear wing has the biggest problem from the point of view of afflux, airflow being broken up and disrupted by the wheels, cockpit fairings and roll-over bar. Of course, F1 dimensional regulations are extremely restrictive and do

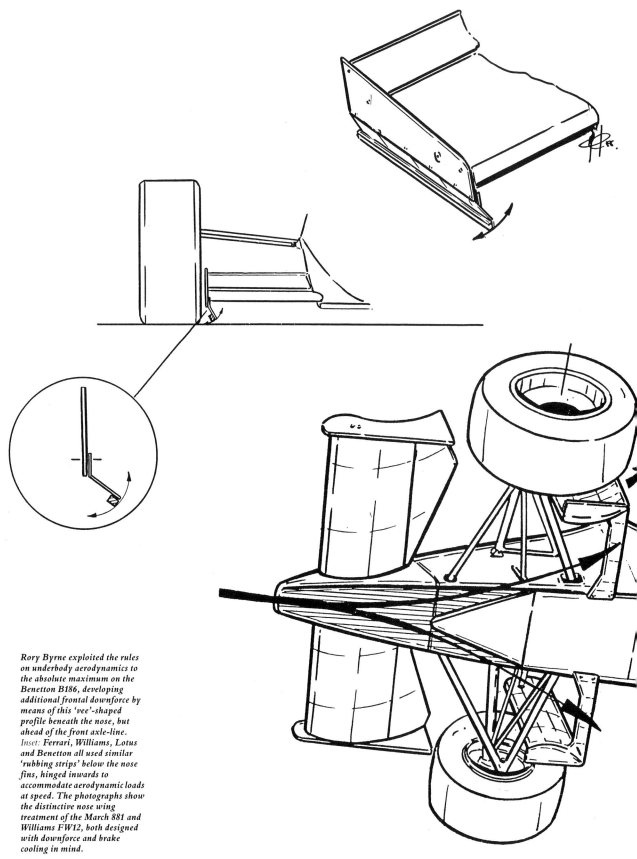

Rory Byrne exploited the rules on underbody aerodynamics to the absolute maximum on the Benetton B186, developing additional frontal downforce by means of this 'vee'-shaped profile beneath the nose, but ahead of the front axle-line. *Inset:* Ferrari, Williams, Lotus and Benetton all used similar 'rubbing strips' below the nose fins, hinged inwards to accommodate aerodynamic loads at speed. The photographs show the distinctive nose wing treatment of the March 881 and Williams FW12, both designed with downforce and brake cooling in mind.

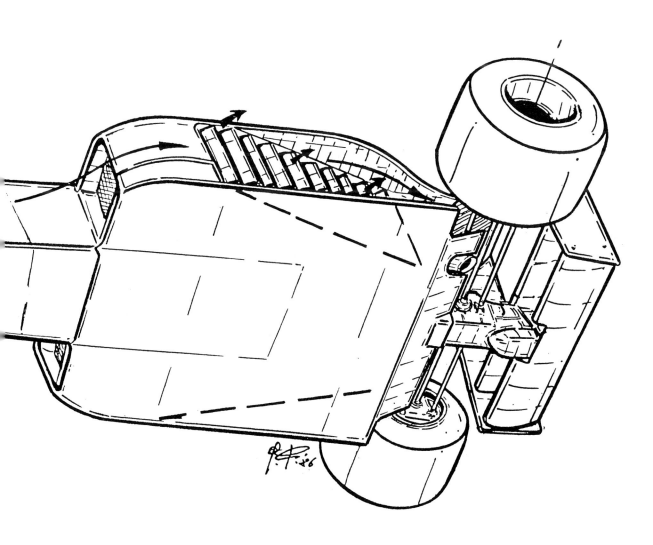

not permit rear wings to be higher than 100 cm from the ground, so there is a restriction on the amount of scope a designer has for raising it to a level where there is no problem with afflux.

When the flat-bottom F1 regulations came into force, McLaren's respected Chief Designer, John Barnard, sought to make up for lost downforce with a distinctively 'waisted' bodywork leading onto rear upturned ramps mounted inside the rear wheels on either side of the gearbox. This proved a major step forward in regaining lost downforce and was soon copied by all his rivals although, interestingly, Barnard retained the large ground-effect side pods to contain water radiators on the Cosworth-engined MP4/1 chassis and, later, all the paraphernalia of intercoolers on the TAG turbo-propelled MP4/2. The retention of these pods hardly compromised the handling of Barnard's machines and Niki Lauda, for one, was extremely glad to have the added protection of those pods round the cockpit area. Not for him the slim centre fuselage...

Most aerodynamic development in recent years has been a question of polishing up a minuscule improvement here and there, perhaps with the result that the car picks up the odd tenth of a second – until, suddenly, you find yourself with an advantage of half a second or so. Engine configuration dictated the effectiveness of a car's aerodynamics to a great extent, a matter to which we shall return in Chapter 5 on integrating the whole design of an F1 car. This was a problem Gordon Murray, in particular, faced over at Brabhams where the four-cylinder BMW turbocharged engine, with its tall cylinder block, defied all efforts to achieve decent airflow over the BT54's rear wing.

'It had struck me for a long time that we were forgetting some fundamental principles of racing car design,' Gordon reflects, 'one of which is that the centre of gravity should be as low as conceivably possible. At the time we were getting rather frustrated with that vertical BMW engine; we could spend a week in the wind tunnel and not find half a second a lap. We started the 1985 season knowing that there wasn't much we could do about it, but Nelson Piquet had been very keen for me to do a low-line car and had been pressing the team on the subject for some while.'

Piquet's preoccupation with reclining the driver as low as possible was something he retained when he moved to Williams in 1986, something which had been fostered during his F3 days when he used to loosen his seat belt on the straight at Silverstone and tuck down another inch or so in the cockpit of his Ralt in order to pick up another couple of hundred revs or more. Being much shorter than Nigel Mansell, Nelson badgered Patrick Head to produce a personalised, special, even lower-line version of the already low FW11B, anxious as he was to capitalise on any advantage over his alleged team-mate. Lest this be construed as nothing more than a minor personal quirk, it should be said that Nigel Mansell became similarly concerned about as low a driving position as possible when *he* discovered that, by driving without a seat in his FW11B and lowering his position in the car by half an inch, a bonus of 50 pounds of additional downforce could be obtained.

Unfortunately, Gordon Murray's ultra-low-line BT55 may have picked up 'between 22 and 32 per cent more downforce' as compared with the previous BT54, but it also developed excessive drag, with the result that it was bog slow in a straight line. However, it was an interesting pointer in the correct theoretical direction and, into 1988, drivers are being reclined more and more in the cockpits in the cause of aerodynamic efficiency.

In many ways, 1987 was something of a turning-point in flat-bottom F1 aerodynamics, the ingenuity of designers and engineers having pretty well clawed back most of the downforce lost when the rules were changed at the start of 1983. In the case of the Williams–Hondas, for example, by the end of '87, the FW11B in its highest downforce trim was developing downloads similar to those the old Cosworth-engined FW08C managed in its fast-circuit, low-downforce guise. Of course, redressing the balance with the FW11B had meant almost doubling the drag in that five-year period, but the additional power of the turbocharged engines helped combat that particular problem.

Facing 1989, designers will be deprived of the prodigious power offered by turbocharged engines. Says Benetton's Pat Symonds, 'I don't think that changes in technical regulations actually make much difference to the amount of wind-tunnel work a team carries out, merely which direction is pursued by the aerodynamicist. With naturally aspirated engines and the current chassis regulations, the aerodynamic areas to concentrate on will be subtly different. But the wind tunnel will continue to be as significant in the design process as it ever has been.'

Small, smooth and compact: the striking Adrian Newey-designed March 881 was one of the most visually attractive cars of the 1988 F1 season.

Chapter 5

Integrating the design

No F1 designer is free to operate totally without constraints. The challenge facing him may involve the adaptation of an existing engine for his 'new' concept, or simply the necessity to build his car to a rigid set of revised technical regulations imposed by the sport's governing body. This happened at the start of 1983 and 1988, for example, when decrees from FISA respectively required a flat-bottomed chassis and the repositioning of the driver's feet *completely* behind the front axle-line. True technical freedom does not – and never has – existed in Grand Prix racing. In fact, when the 1988 chassis regulations were introduced, I asked Gordon Murray what he thought of them. His reply was wry and to the point. 'They are about making all the cars look the same,' he grinned. Looking at the grid in Rio at the start of 1988, it was not difficult to understand what he meant.

Of course, the engine is the overwhelmingly crucial factor in the equation. As a starting-point, let's reflect on the proliferation of 'special builders' that populated the back of the Grand Prix grids in the mid-1970s. Their fortunes were inextricably entwined with the Ford–Cosworth DFV which, although continually undergoing progressive internal specification changes, remained throughout that time the ultimate 'plug it in, fire it up' proprietary Grand Prix power unit.

Remember the Token, Trojan, Maki, Amon, Lec, Connew and a multitude of other small-timers? They may not have set the world on fire, but it was the participation of these sort of people that ensured there was hardly a racing backwater into which knowledge of Cosworth DFV engine installation techniques had not percolated. Versatile and virtually bullet-proof for all practical purposes, its essential dimensions remained unchanged for the twelve years separating its triumphant debut in the 1967 Dutch Grand Prix from the moment when the Williams team, in the interests of ground-effect chassis design, asked for the fuel pump to be repositioned on their engines in 1979.

By the end of the 1970s, the Cosworth DFV element of the design equation could be taken fairly well for granted as the ground-effect era got into full swing. In retrospect, it was probably just as well for the designers' workloads that the challenge of getting the best out of ground effect was not made even more complicated by the necessity to develop totally new engine installations and systems at the same time. Aside from Renault, who were faced with the challenge of evolving both engine and chassis at a time when

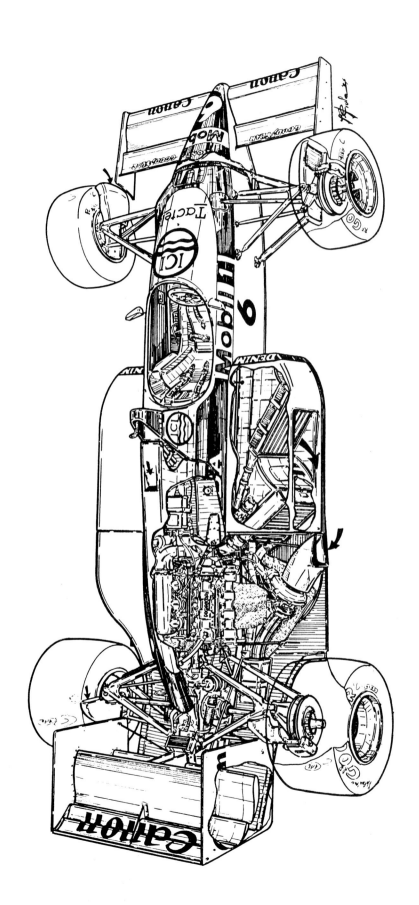

the tempo of Grand Prix technology was speeding up quite dramatically, the problem of turbo-engine installation was still a couple of years down the road for most top-line teams. For the moment, the Cosworth V8 gave people what they needed: a tough, practical and easily serviceable engine which one didn't have to worry about.

One classic example of the way in which an integrated design steadily developed from a complex compromise to one of the most efficient packages in the F1 business can be seen by the evolution of the Patrick Head-designed Williams–Hondas. Starting with the FW09 at the tail end of 1983 the line continued through to the FW11/FW11B which won nine out of the sixteen races in both 1986 and '87, taking the Constructors' title both years.

When the Williams–Honda partnership was forged, there was no element of choice facing Head and his colleagues on the design staff at Williams GP Engineering. While his old friend John Barnard had been allowed the luxury of a totally clean sheet of paper on which to enumerate his design requirements for the TAG-financed, Porsche-built V6 twin-turbo engine which was destined to dominate the 1984 Championship battle, Head inherited the lumpy, untidy-looking 80-degree Japanese V6 which had grown out of Honda's 2-litre F2 unit. Briefly fielded by the tiny Spirit team in a handful of races during the second half of 1983, the Honda V6 came to Williams with no instructions for installation, advice or significant technical input. Spirit had not really learned a great deal, apart from the fact that the engine was temperamental and, at this stage at least, rather unreliable. Head and Co. now had to start from scratch.

It was a major challenge for the Didcot team. By the end of 1983 the taut, compact little DFV-engined FW08C had been refined to a superb pitch. The team and drivers knew every facet of its make-up in precise and specific detail. Now, midway through the 1983 racing season, Patrick had to tear himself away from the week-to-week challenge of racing to produce a brand new chassis for a brand new engine. The decision was taken that the FW09 should make its debut at the last race of the year, the South African Grand Prix, the idea being that the winter break could then be used to massage the new car into a properly competitive challenger for 1984. That was the idea, anyway...

The story of the FW09 underlines just what a complex jigsaw the development of a Grand Prix car can turn into, each element of its performance inextricably entwined with several others to the point where a theoretical improvement in one area can produce a frustrating step backwards in another. I well recall sitting on the pit barrier with Keke Rosberg during practice for that Kyalami race, chatting to him about the prospects for 1984 and the new car.

'I reckon we are in a very strong position indeed,' he enthused, 'because our car is ready early, my contract is all tied up and I don't have to worry about what might and might not happen next season. I'm feeling very relaxed about the future and, although the car has a touch too much understeer for my taste, I'm pretty sure this is just a question of putting a few more miles onto it. It just needs more development testing.' Within eight months, Rosberg would not be feeling so charitable towards the FW09, even though he was able to coax a superb win at Dallas out of the car, the first triumph for the Williams–Honda partnership.

117

What had lured the drivers into making approving noises about the car's handling at Kyalami was the fact that there was insufficient intercooling capacity which, in turn, meant that the Honda engines could not be run with as much boost pressure as was theoretically possible. Moreover, in the rush to complete the cars in time for the race, they were fitted with FW08 transmissions and rocker-arm rear suspension.

As more effective intercooling was developed during the winter, thanks to a typically intensive bout of wind-tunnel testing by Frank Dernie, so Patrick Head concentrated on a new rear-end set-up for the car. A totally new gearbox mated to pullrod activation of the coil-spring/damper units was evolved in the interests of improved adhesion, but that additional rear-end grip simply aggravated the 'slight understeer' problem into a major shortcoming which, if Keke's comments were anything to go by, made the car an absolute anathema to him. Better intercooling, of course, allowed more boost to be used, in turn unlocking more usable power and, with the Honda V6's fierce power characteristics with a tremendous surge at a certain point in the rev range, the understeer problem was ever more aggravated.

Meanwhile, Patrick Head had studied the neat waisted rear end which had been employed on the McLarens during 1983 and concluded that it would be a worthwhile feature to adopt on the FW09, theoretically offering more downforce without the penalty of additional drag. However, there was no way in which these distinctive aerodynamic 'ramps' could be meshed into the design within the constraints of a pullrod suspension system, so a return was made to the FW08-style rocker-arm rear end, in time for tests prior to the Detroit/Montreal mid-season races. The rear end, though, was simply too crowded for the whole arrangement to be packaged properly, so the FW09s went back to their pullrod rear ends for the North American tour. Thereafter, the wheelbase was lengthened by 5 inches, allowing the waisted rear end and revamped transmission package to be fitted without problem, and these FW09Bs ran out the remainder of the 1984 season.

Head decided to start with a clean sheet of paper for 1985, even though he did not fully share Rosberg's opinion that the FW09's basic problem had been a flexing chassis. There had been a slight problem with flexing cylinder blocks, to which Honda's R & D department addressed itself over the winter, but Patrick remained convinced that it was all basically a matter of the newness of the Williams–Honda relationship. Moreover, if Honda could do something to 'soften' the power curve, then there would be improvements all round, since an increase in driver acceptance would be accompanied by benefits for the inherent chassis balance.

Mid-season, Honda came up with their 'E' spec. version of the V6 which delivered its not inconsiderable power in more progressive fashion, instantly to be praised by both the team's drivers. In time for the GP of Europe, the engine cover was lowered thanks to the fitting of a smaller, lower plenum chamber to the Honda engine. This 10-cm reduction in the height of the engine cover significantly improved the airflow over the rear wing which, in addition to the new pullrod rear suspension (the FW10s had been fitted with rocker-arm suspension throughout the season up to that point) made a significant improvement to the car's handling and traction. A new gearbox casing was fitted on which the suspension mounting points were attached, replacing the separate framework which was previously employed.

The arrival of the 195-litre fuel capacity regulations led Head to produce yet another brand new car, the FW11, which was to become the basis of the definitive Williams–Honda and, for 1987, the team would rely on an evolutionary 'B' version of this machine. Williams by now had the benefit of a very expensive computer-aided design/manufacturing (CAD/CAM) facility, the General Electric CALMA system.

The FW11 design represented a turning-point in the progress of Williams design/manufacturing techniques, the superbly made carbon-composite chassis setting fresh standards for detail finish and precise fitting of components which have outlasted the Honda collaboration. They continue to manifest themselves in the compact Judd-engined FW12 used by Mansell and Patrese in 1988. Truly integrated designs assume a new dimension when one starts to consider the potential offered by such systems.

Talking to *Autosport* at the start of the 1988 F1 season, Frank Dernie put the system's potential into clear perspective, but warned: 'It's only a tool, an aid to design. It won't make a bad engineer good...' But, that said, the facility

The first product of the Williams–Honda alliance was the FW09, seen here being hurried by Keke Rosberg to a memorable victory at Dallas in 1984. Very much a development machine, it taught Patrick Head and his engineering team a great deal about the essentials of turbo technology.

to come up with a 3-D picture on the computer screen and experiment with various different design ideas without ever having to make any components until you are satisfied that every aspect of the concept is ideally suited to your needs, makes for much more efficient and rewarding use of an engineer's precious time. 'The conceptual stuff comes first,' explains Dernie, 'so the first thing you do is to think about it, then use the computer to come up with it and look at it on the screen, checking radiator ducts, for example, or deciding whether you'd like to try a new rear wing, or whatever.

'When you are happy with that, you create quarter-scale drawings which the model-maker uses to create a wind-tunnel model. Having gone through all that, we wind-tunnel test the model and, if a particular idea shows promise – an isolated bit, perhaps simply a front wing or nose duct – it may well be taken in isolation and moved onto the team's current car. If it's a conceptual layout, of course, like moving the radiator into the rear wing, then clearly you are thinking in terms of a totally new car. Of course, it may be changes to the structure that are being considered, or a new suspension layout, for example.

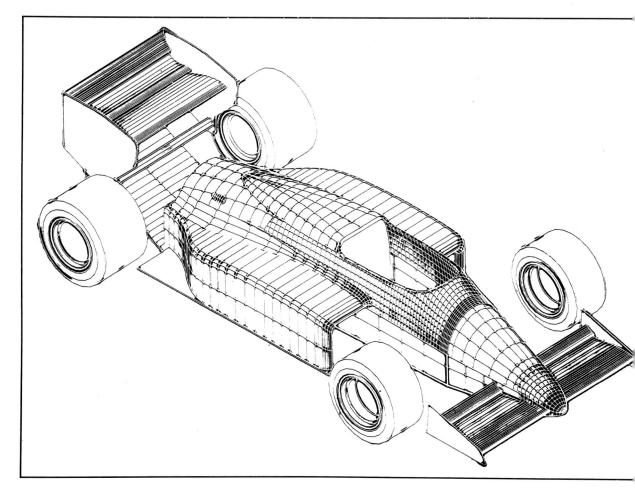

'If there are problems once the model has got into the wind tunnel – say a radiator duct doesn't work – then you can either scrap it or perhaps you might conclude "Well, it works OK at the top, but not at the bottom" so we just go back to the workstation, redesign it on the computer, have a drawing in a few minutes, take it along to the model-maker and get the wind-tunnel model revised accordingly. Before, we would try to do it with bits of sticky tape, cardboard and lumps of filler and then have the problem of measuring the effectiveness of those modifications when we got it back into the wind tunnel.'

Once the basic shape is finalised, the next thing is to decide on the length of the monocoque, the positioning of the bulkheads – at which point Patrick Head takes over the design process to detail the intricacies of *how* the chassis is to be assembled and in what manner the carbon-composite materials will be laid up.

Employing such CAD/CAM systems leads quite logically to the area of finite element stressing – put simply, a detailed structural analysis of the complex composite parts, 'to see what we can get away with, if you like' says Dernie. However, to produce really accurate results in this area will take far, far longer than perhaps the Williams design team initially anticipated.

Computer-aided design (CAD/CAM) facilities are an increasingly indispensable tool of the contemporary F1 chassis designer. Images produced in this way (below left) *helped finalise the lines of the Ferrari F187 for 1987 and '88.*

'You could do the job quickly,' continues Dernie, 'but it would not accurately verify anything, so would therefore be a waste of time. If you get to within 30 per cent of an accurate answer, you really have a bloody good result. With a racing chassis, with the honeycomb, layers of composites, different angles of fibres, you're dealing with an outstandingly complicated structure. If you use too coarse an FE mesh in a critical area, your error can be hundreds of per cent. With our team's experience of composites, we already know what not to do, so you are really better off not using FE analysis until you can do the job properly, and be confident of the results from test pieces and so on. You might just as well use experience under these circumstances, although FE analysis is definitely one of our major goals.'

Having said that, Williams does already use FE analysis for various metal components in their cars. 'For example, on the hydraulics for our active suspension, the pressure vessels, the accumulator and the struts, all the parts we designed ourselves – but not, of course, for things like pipes and hoses which were bought off the shelf. Another example of how it helped the team was in 1986 when we broke a CV joint in the Austrian Grand Prix, so we just stuck the cage on the computer, looked at various loading conditions and used the information to redesign the cage. Now we make our own!'

So the advantages of a CAD/CAM system are several and varied. It's much quicker. You get nice clean drawings and, as Dernie reminds us, there is that wonderful facility of being able to work in three dimensions.

'I wanted to make the body of the FW11, for example, as small as possible,' he explained, 'but the Honda engine is *gargantuan* compared to the European engines such as the Renault or TAG, to take just two. Also, the Honda's basic layout, with all the bracketry too, was crude and it proved quite a job to fit it all in.

'So it was fantastic to be able to take, say, the engine management box in 3D, and then take sections and check clearances and even be able to show that we would have to remove some of the engine cover honeycomb to make it fit! Before, of course, that was all done by the mechanics during assembly; now it's all done before we start making the car. Much of the time in the prototype shop can be saved.

'You can take sections and say "That's quite a good space, we can put the water pipes through there" or "The gear linkage is going to foul here". Being able to look at things in quite substantial detail before you cut metal obviously saves you time and money.

'It also gives you all your dimensions automatically and doesn't generate drawing errors unless you force it to do so – in the old days, for example, a draughtsman might have wanted a one-quarter-inch hole, but drew a one-eighth-inch hole by accident. That can't happen. It's almost self-checking, so errors are easier to spot!'

Slashing the permissible fuel load from 220 to 195 litres also enabled the drivers to adopt a laid-back driving position, about 4 inches lower. This configuration was retained for the 1987 FW11Bs – the first time Williams had used an 'evolutionary' car since the turbo era began – but although the later cars were visually almost identical, Frank Dernie acknowledged with some satisfaction that 'they developed more downforce for no increase in drag...' Predictably, he was reluctant to say *how much* more downforce was developed by the 1987 Williams.

The Williams FW12's clean lines were developed with the assistance of GEC Calma CAD/CAM design facilities at the team's Didcot factory.

122

John Barnard's superbly integrated MP4–TAG design stood the test of time marvellously. Introduced at the end of 1983, it evolved into the car which is seen here at Adelaide, more than three years later, carrying Alain Prost to victory and to his second World Championship title.

Honing the Williams–Honda package to perfection was a process which took a full four seasons, the technical combination reaching its peak level of achievement in only the third and fourth years. The 1984 and '85 challenges were blunted by the fact that Patrick Head and his design team had been forced into a learning process at double-quick time, with basic equipment that was always going to be something of a compromise. That the two partners did such an impressive job in the end is a tribute to the amount of finance, personnel and technical ingenuity brought to bear on the engine development programme by Honda, allied to the clever, precise and wholly reliable engineering standards established for the cars by Patrick Head's design team at Williams GPE.

In terms of integrating the overall design, Williams took those two seasons to reach the level that the superb John Barnard-designed TAG-engined McLarens started from in 1984. The irony for Williams, of course, was that their detailed work on Honda engine installation became the 'standard package' once the Japanese firm decided to provide engines for Lotus as from the start of 1987. Their carefully evolved engine installation package was handed to Lotus 'on a plate' as a reward for four seasons of experimentation and development.

A similar 'standard package' of carefully worked out water radiators and intercoolers was produced by Renault when the French company expanded the supply of its V6 engines, first to embrace Lotus in 1983 and later Ligier and Tyrrell in '84 and '85 respectively. This took the element of experimentation out of the equation for the customer teams, who could rely on a fixed specification engine/intercooler set-up, a level of dependability not experienced since the days of the 'plug-in' Cosworth DFV. Needless to say the 'customers', in the form of Team Lotus, very quickly began doing a better job than the 'supplier' when it came to producing a chassis/engine combination.

By contrast, John Barnard's 'clean-sheet' concept worked brilliantly from the outset. Having considered, and rejected, just about every available turbocharged engine for McLaren International's big step forward into the forced induction era, there was only one logical course of action to adopt – commission somebody to build a brand new engine from the sump up, one which would absolutely conform to Barnard's chassis installation requirements. The 'somebody' approached on the subject was Porsche, who showed a great deal of interest in a commercial arrangement whereby McLaren financed the production of a Grand Prix engine strictly conforming to Barnard's rigorous design parameters and specifications.

At the time the engine was originally commissioned, ground-effect chassis installation considerations were of absolutely paramount importance. Therefore, Barnard's requirements were based round a narrow engine – certainly with nothing bigger than a 90-degree vee – with exhaust pipes raised sufficiently to clear the aerodynamic underfloors as they swept upwards towards the tail of the car. Water and oil pumps would have to be positioned at the front of the car, the engine had to be a stressed member, and so on.

Then came one of those stroke-of-the-pen regulation changes for which FISA has gained such notoriety over the years: in November 1982, the sport's governing body announced that flat-bottomed cars would be obligatory as from the start of the 1983 season. Barnard's original concept of the ultimate turbocharged ground-effect Grand Prix challenger now lay

McLaren International's drawing office at the team's new Woking factory. High-tech and ever-higher standards.

BMW's M12/13 four-cylinder turbo engine was revamped specifically for angled installation in the Brabham BT55 chassis.

in tatters. He was left with an engine, elements of which would not have been designed the way they had if John had been seeking to produce a flat-bottomed Grand Prix design from day one.

The Hercules carbon-composite tub, round which the soon-to-be-titled TAG turbos were installed, owed much to Barnard's original MP4 concept that hit the tracks in 1981, powered by a naturally aspirated Cosworth DFV engine. In fact, the first TAG-engined test car was a modified MP4/1 and the first two turbo race cars, in effect updated development machines, were also built up round modified MP4/1C monocoques and labelled 'MP4/1E' for their late season '83 outings. This went very much against the grain for Barnard, who originally counselled that the DFV-engined cars should be raced through to the end of the season while the TAG turbo was developed quietly, off-stage, in preparation for a race debut the following year.

At the start of the 1984 season, having produced the 'definitive' first-generation TAG-engined design, Barnard and McLaren were 'last out of the box' with their new car relative to their front-running rivals. Barnard's insistence on researching every element of the design in microscopic detail before giving the green light to build the cars imposed a huge strain on the McLaren workforce, but usually ended up with the right answer from the start. John's McLaren–TAG came straight out of the factory to win in Brazil in '84, Alain Prost in the cockpit, a success that was repeated the following year, and then again in 1987 and '88 with brand new post-Barnard McLarens, TAG- and Honda-engined respectively.

That Barnard's design was properly integrated from the start in 1984 was evidenced by the fact that relatively few changes were made to the MP4/2 throughout that breathtaking 1984 season, when Prost and Niki Lauda won twelve of the season's sixteen World Championship qualifying rounds. Significant alterations included a new front wing package in time for the Austrian Grand Prix and an enlarged turbo air intake on the rear bodywork, but the basic concept of the car remained unchanged and there was no necessity to build a brand new car for 1985.

This allowed Barnard to refine the basic package for the defence of the team's Constructors' title, concentrating on serviceability and reliability. The MP4/2 was updated to conform with the new footbox regulations which imposed mandatory crash-testing requirements before acceptance. Pullrod rear suspension and new hubs and suspension uprights were also incorporated, together with new bodywork and revised aerodynamics to make up for the

126

banning of the additional 'winglets', fitted within the wheelbase of the car, which had originally been introduced by Ferrari in 1983 and were then copied by all and sundry the following season.

In 1985 the MP4/2B won five Grands Prix in Prost's hands and one in Lauda's, despite a switch from Michelin to Goodyear rubber, foisted on McLaren after the French firm's withdrawal. Again, no major changes were made to the package during the course of the year, although subtly repositioned front suspension pick-up points were required to rectify a worrying mid-season handling imbalance.

Again, into 1986, the basic recipe continued unchanged, although a smaller 195-litre fuel cell enabled the driver to sit lower in the cockpit, in a more reclined position. The MP4/2C carried Prost to his second straight Championship and, even when Barnard left McLaren at the end of 1986, the design team that succeeded him produced an MP4/3 which was still a generic development not only of the very first TAG-engined car, but of the original MP4 which had first seen the light of day back in 1981. 'Make it right and it will last for years,' Barnard used to smile. As an example of a fully integrated F1 design which was bang on target from the start, the McLaren–TAGs have had few peers in F1's recent history.

With the end of the turbo era scheduled for the close of the 1988 Grand Prix season, naturally aspirated 3.5-litre engines were allowed into the F1 business from the start of 1987, the idea being to allow a period of transition for those teams who wanted to make the switch early, either for technical or financial reasons. In 1987, with the turbos still running at 4-bar boost pressure on 195 litres, the naturally aspirated brigade amounted to a handful of teams, all of whom had been driven to contesting F1's 'second division' simply because they could not contemplate the financial commitment to turbocharged engines for what was clearly a very limited competitive life. In order to stimulate some interest, FISA initiated the Jim Clark and Colin Chapman Cups for drivers and constructors of such naturally aspirated machinery, Jonathan Palmer and the Tyrrell team respectively winning these inconsequential consolation prizes.

However, in the second transitional season prior to their demise, the 1988 technical regulations imposed what looked like swingeing restrictions on turbocharged engines, reducing the permissible boost level to 2.5-bar and the fuel capacity to 150 litres. This was in line with FISA's self-confessed intention of loading the dice very heavily in favour of the naturally aspirated cars, a decision which rather underestimated the amount of effort that Honda and Ferrari, in particular, were prepared to spend on engine development in order to keep their forced induction engines in play.

None the less, the quality of the naturally aspirated contenders proved greatly enhanced, with such notable names as Williams and Benetton switching to that route and, together with a number of machines from other teams, dramatically upping the tempo of technical development and clever design packaging. Williams, having found itself dropped by Honda, picked up a programme based round the newly developed 3.5-litre Judd V8, this power unit also being adopted by Ligier and March who abandoned Megatron turbo and Cosworth–Ford DFZ power respectively. Benetton switched to using the new Cosworth–Ford DFR engine, not because it lacked a turbo, but because Cosworth and Ford jointly came to the decision that it

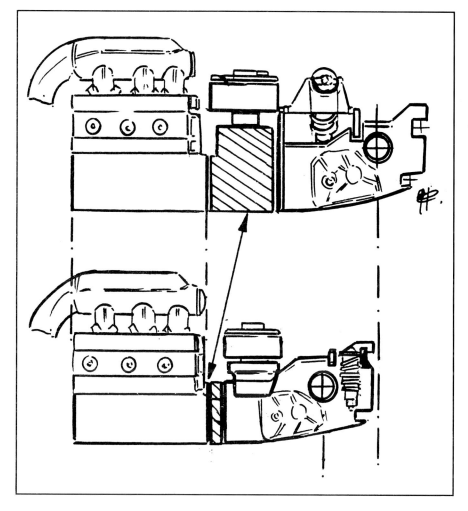

A question of packaging. This Giorgio Piola drawing indicates the changes Ferrari made to the rear of their 1985 car in order to vary its wheelbase during the course of the season. The upper drawing shows the long wheelbase configuration with the oil tank atop the bellhousing; the lower, the short wheelbase layout with an ultra-short bellhousing and the oil tank on top of the gearbox.

would be uneconomic to invest in the necessary work to make their 120-degree turbo operate to best effect under the new boost and fuel capacity regulations.

The constructional regulations were changed quite significantly as well. Turbo teams which wanted to continue running their 1987 machinery were permitted to do so, as long as they *were* really to the same specification. On that count, Ferrari, Arrows, Zakspeed and Osella qualified, but McLaren didn't, because it had switched from TAG to Honda engines. New cars – and all naturally aspirated contenders – had to conform to stringent new constructional requirements.

In addition to crash testing the nose box, new monocoques also had to be subjected to a side impact, something which caused some minor design changes 'on the way' for some teams that were building totally new cars. The chassis side members, running the length of the cockpit, also had to be uprated in specification to form an additional protective barrier, and the soles of the drivers' feet, upright on the pedals, now had to be positioned completely behind the centreline of the front wheels.

With the naturally aspirated cars allowed a minimum weight limit 40 kg inside that of the turbos, an advantage negated in part by the necessity to start races with a fuel load about 30 litres in excess of the turbo cars, there was a premium on clever packaging and aerodynamic efficiency as seldom before. In that respect, Williams and Ligier toiled away over the winter in an effort to come up with the perfect technical solution, based round the Judd engine. As things transpired, no two cars sharing an identical power unit could have turned out to be more dissimilar.

Drawing from his experiences with the FW11 series Honda-engined cars, Patrick Head's FW12 concept was an uncomplicated, yet ultra-compact chassis which was based round the use of the Williams computer-controlled 'reactive' suspension system, a refinement of that used by Piquet to win the Italian GP at Monza the previous autumn.

Activated by pushrods, the tiny hydraulic jacks were mounted atop the front of the monocoque, completely clear of the driver's footwell. The tiny hydraulic rams were tucked away beneath an access hatch on top of the chassis, activated by pushrods at the front, while at the rear the rams were mounted tight in behind the transverse gearbox, and moved by a pullrod arrangement. The side pods were extremely compact and, indeed, in the sweltering Rio heat needed some *ad hoc* surgery in order that the Judd engine received sufficient cooling, while the 190-litre cell was completely packaged behind the driver, its most forward extremity being the rear wall of the cockpit. Head wanted to have no truck with packaging fuel in a tank which in any way 'wrapped round' the driver's seat, although this was an option favoured by several of his rivals. Topped off by that splendid transverse six-speed gearbox, reputedly weighing a mere 40 per cent of the six-speeder used on the FW11–Honda, the FW12 was a masterpiece of cleverly integrated Grand Prix car design: logical, uncluttered and lacking in unnecessary complexity.

Over at Ligier, Michel Tetu resolved to bury painful memories of the floundering Megatron-engined JS29 which had proved such a consistently disappointing contender throughout 1987. Starting with a clean sheet of paper, Tetu came up with what superficially looked like one of the most visually attractive cars of 1988. At least, until its bodywork was removed... critics accused him of ignoring one of racing car design's golden rules: never produce something over-complex when there is the alternative of taking a straightforward route. With the laudable aim of positioning the Judd engine in the *centre* of the car, Tetu divided the fuel load between 120 litres in what amounted to a seat and wrap-round side tank, and a separate 70-litre tank positioned *between* the engine and gearbox, further down towards the back of the car.

Before embarking on this scheme, Tetu approached FISA for guidance. Although many rival designers raised their eyebrows when they saw that the rearward fuel cell was a separate unit, not part of the main monocoque, FISA nodded its approval. The general paddock consensus may have been that the fuel cells should be 'within the main structure', but where was there a definition of the main structure? Not in the F1 technical regulations, apparently, so Tetu 'borrowed' from the F3000 regulations, which define the main structure as that part of the car joining the front and rear wheels. FISA let it through, perhaps anticipating that it would not turn out to be the electrifying pace-setter that Ligier may have been hoping for.

To balance out the rearmost fuel reservoir, the Ligier's front fuel cells ran so far forward along the cockpit sides as to give rise to some fears over their vulnerability in the event of a heavy impact pushing one of the front wheels back in towards the side of the chassis. However, these reservations notwithstanding, the JS31 was an extremely slender piece of equipment, its spring/dampers tucked tightly inboard front and rear, activated by pushrod and pullrod respectively.

Sadly, initial testing found the car to be a real handful and, despite the fact that a preferential drainage facility had been incorporated into the design, the car proved 'nervous' and almost impossible to balance out to the drivers' taste. First impressions suggested that, masterpiece of packaging though it might have looked, the fundamental concept was too complex and, more to the point, too *heavy* for it to be immediately competitive.

An enormously wide variety of suspension packages could be seen on this new generation of super-efficient GP machines. The number one priority was to position the coil-spring/damper units so as to cause the absolute minimum of disruption to the aerodynamic efficiency of the front end. But this was only part of a wider challenge. There was also the need to produce the optimum weight distribution within the chosen wheelbase, for the new technical regulations had obliged designers to move the drivers back some 15 inches or so to provide for the new footwell regulations.

The McLaren MP4/4 is the only example of the new 1988 breed to retain the coil-spring/damper units tucked inside the front of the monocoque, activated by pushrods. Fellow-Honda turbo-users, Lotus, opted to mount the 100T's spring/dampers atop the monocoque above the driver's feet, thereby allowing much more space within the footwell, a configuration also adopted by the Lola LC88. The net result for these two cars is that the front bodywork ahead of the cockpit appears quite high and bulbous.

If you don't want to clutter up the footwell, or crowd the top of the monocoque, Tyrrell, Rial and Benetton all offer yet more options as far as the positioning of those spring/dampers are concerned. Keen to retain the striking 'needle nose' which had become such a distinctive trademark of his recent F1 designs, Rory Byrne decided to package the spring/dampers across the car, but *beneath* the driver's heels. They are operated via a bell crank which, in turn, is activated by pullrods, a package which Rory believes assists the aerodynamic efficiency of the front end of the car.

Rial's designer, Gustav Brunner, has laid the spring/dampers of his neat new ARC1 along the lower edge of the monocoque, lying parallel to the centreline of the car, and again activated by pullrods. On the Tyrrell 017, designer Brian Lisles has helped keep the front of the monocoque as ultra-slim as possible by hanging the spring/dampers on the outside of the chassis, although the position of the front axle-line has made it necessary to angle the pullrods forward quite sharply from the top end of the fabricated upright to the bottom of the shock absorber.

It remains one of the most tantalising and absorbing elements of Grand Prix racing that, from so many disparate starting-points, and incorporating so many detailed idiosyncrasies, these widely differing packages come together to produce a track performance ending up a mere few tenths of a second apart.

Star of the show. The McLaren–Honda MP4/4 proved to be another outstanding performer from the Woking-based team, proving unbeatable during the first half of the 1988 championship season.

THE DESIGNERS

John Barnard

Architect behind the magnificent McLaren–TAGs which powered Niki Lauda (1984) and Alain Prost (1985 and 1986) to a hat-trick of World Championship titles, John Barnard left the McLaren International team in the autumn of 1986 to take on a dramatic new challenge. Head-hunted by Ferrari, he signed with the Italian team as Technical Director, but with one unique proviso: he didn't want to work in Italy.

Such a request may have been regarded as heresy by dyed-in-the-wool *Ferrariste,* but Barnard's wish was granted. He established a Ferrari satellite outpost, titled Guildford Technical Office, in an ultra-modern new complex at Shalford, a few miles from Guildford. It was a tribute to his reputation as well as his refusal to be deflected from any path he passionately wished to pursue.

Barnard's recent reputation with McLaren International and the TAG-engined cars sometimes makes one forget that John achieved quite a fair amount before he struck up that partnership with Ron Dennis back in 1980. Born in 1946, he was always incredibly enthusiastic about cars, even though his first job with GEC, designing machines for making electric light bulbs, might not have suggested a career in motor racing design was beckoning. However, in 1968 he inquired of both Lola and McLaren whether there were any jobs going.

Ironically, McLaren's Jo Marquart suggested he gain more experience with minor-league machinery before aspiring to join a Grand Prix team, but John found a more receptive reaction from Eric Broadley at Lola and was immediately offered a job in the drawing office. John Barnard was on his way . . .

In retrospect, there could hardly have been a better opportunity around. At the time, Lola was producing cars for just about every conceivable international and domestic racing category, offering the aspiring designer enormous scope for a wide variety of work. It was at this powerhouse of race car production that Patrick Head also surfaced as one of Barnard's contemporaries, later designing the Williams F1 cars which would shape up against Barnard's McLarens more than ten years afterwards.

During his four years with Lola, Barnard's design efforts included work on Formula Fords and Super Vees and, later, the T280-DFV and T290-FVC sports cars, plus input into the T260 Can-Am design which Jackie Stewart drove in 1971 against the might of the factory McLarens. Then, in 1972, John

Barnard got his first F1 break.

A post became vacant at McLaren, so John was in like a flash to assume what amounted to a number two role alongside Gordon Coppuck, then in the final stages of pencilling the superb M23 design which would carry Emerson Fittipaldi and James Hunt to World Championships in 1974 and 1976 respectively. John did a lot of work on the detailed monocoque design for this new car, but his perfectionist streak, which would harden into an uncompromising and extremely strong will by the time he made it to the top with the McLaren–TAGs, found it very difficult to come to terms with the receptive, wide-open approach towards design which was practised by the Colnbrook-based team in the early 1970s. A legacy of the late Bruce McLaren's gentle, tolerant style, Barnard could not accept it as easily as the relaxed Coppuck, feeling that a Chief Designer should be just that, not subject to input from the factory floor.

John's design work also included producing the neat M25 F5000 car – an F1 M23, in effect, with its Chevy V8 installed as a stressed member – while he found it a particular challenge to work on the late model M16 Indy cars, redesigning the internal monocoque components for the M16E in order to reduce weight and stiffen it up. Then came another major career opportunity, this time in the USA.

Barnard received an approach to work for the Vel's Parnelli Indy car team, based at Parnelli's headquarters in Torrance, California. He went out there in July 1975 as successor to Maurice Philippe, later Tyrrell's Chief Designer, and worked briefly on the beautiful VPJ4 Formula 1 car which was being driven by Mario Andretti. However, the team's main priority was the Indy car, so John concentrated on developing the VPJ6B to the point where it became acknowledged as the most advanced design in the business in 1976, Al Unser speeding to victories at Pocono, Milwaukee and Phoenix.

Unhappily, the Vel's Parnelli team was disbanded at the end of 1977, but Al Unser put John in touch with Chaparral boss Jim Hall, who was keen to produce a new Indy car project. Barnard initiated a ground-effect concept, the design and manufacture of which he convinced Hall would be better executed in the UK due to the wider availability of the specialist skills required. John actually designed the car in his father's house in North Wembley, the finished product being built by B&S Fabrications, the specialist fabrications company which would eventually do some component work on the prototype chassis to take the 3.5-litre V12 naturally aspirated Ferrari F1 engine which came on the scene in 1988.

Sadly, although Al Unser led the Indy 500 commandingly in Barnard's new creation, the media seldom gave much credit to John's design efforts, most of the praise accruing to Jim Hall despite the fact that Barnard's original agreement had stipulated due acknowledgement of his contribution. They split up, John thereafter freelancing until Ron Dennis approached him in November 1979, with a proposal to design a new F1 machine for his Project 4 operation.

Dennis's close links with Marlboro eventually led, quite logically, to the amalgamation of Project 4 and the McLaren team, by then in a pretty parlous state with not a win to its credit since 1977. John's role in the new consortium was to be that of Chief Designer, although he was a little wary of McLaren's 'consensus' design process and had to put his foot down in quite

John Watson, ready to go in one of Barnard's MP4/1Bs. In 1982 he won the Belgian and Detroit Grands Prix with this machine.

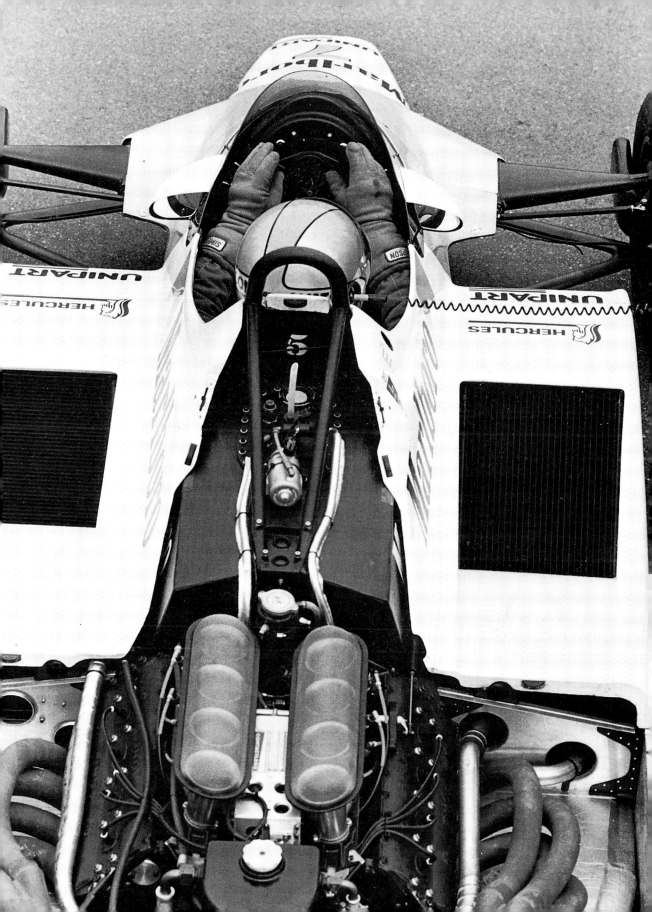

*Grand partnership: Barnard
(left), Lauda and Prost conspired
to take the World Championship
by storm in 1984, '85 and '86.*

a big way. But everything worked out reasonably well.

John's new F1 project, the MP4/1 was, of course, the first Grand Prix car to have its chassis manufactured out of carbon-fibre composite materials. A contact at BAC had given him an insight into what was possible with CFC and John immediately realised its enormous potential for F1 purposes. That said, he was disappointed that he could find no enthusiasm for his ideas among the specialist companies who could have helped the manufacturing process in the UK. 'It was very dispiriting,' he recalls.

However, one of Barnard's friends in the USA suggested he approach Hercules Inc., the aerospace specialists in Salt Lake City who had considerable experience of working with CFC. Dennis and Barnard made a telephone call out of the blue, got through to the right guy and, to their mutual relief, received the thumbs-up. A deal was struck for Hercules to make the CFC monocoques, after which they were shipped to the McLaren factory at Woking to be built into completed cars.

The first MP4/1 hit the tracks at the start of the 1981 season, its elegant aerodynamics and high build quality standing as a testimony to Barnard's meticulous approach. It won the British Grand Prix in John Watson's hands, thereby returning McLaren to the winner's circle for the first time in almost four seasons. In 1982 the team won four races, in 1983 there was just a lone triumph at Long Beach, with the Cosworth-engined cars. But, long term, there was something much more exciting up John Barnard's sleeve – the

TAG-propelled McLaren MP4/2s which would hold sway in F1 for three glorious seasons.

Although eventually they found it impossible to continue working together, Barnard and Dennis were a superbly matched partnership. On design and managerial fronts respectively, each was a perfectionist in his own area. So when it was decided to approach Porsche to build a purpose-made turbocharged F1 engine, both men harboured similar ambitions. Once Dennis had secured the necessary finance with which to underpin the project, Barnard outlined his list of requirements to the Porsche engineering team.

The result was probably the most integrated F1 design of the turbo era, even though the compact external dimensions of the TAG V6 were originally laid down by Barnard with ground-effect underbody technology in mind when Porsche was commissioned to build it in 1982. By the time it arrived on the scene, FISA's new regulations decreed that flat undersides were compulsory.

The racing record of Barnard's McLaren–TAGs needs no recounting here, except in the most cursory detail. They won 12 out of 16 races in 1984, with Niki Lauda taking the Championship, while Prost buttoned up the 1985 and '86 titles with five and three race wins per respective season. Lauda also won one more race in '85 before his retirement.

However, by the time of Prost's second successive crown in Adelaide at the end of 1986, Barnard had left his position at the helm of the McLaren International design team. Having established an autocratic regime which delivered the goods, he began to tire of the challenge.

'I was finding it extremely difficult to sustain my motivation by the middle of the '86 season,' he admitted, 'because the team had been at the top of

John Barnard's TAG-propelled McLaren MP4/2B sustained the team's winning momentum throughout 1985, allowing Alain Prost to win his first Drivers' championship as well as earning a second Constructors' crown for this chassis/engine combination.

the tree for three seasons and the whole thing seemed as though it had developed its own momentum. I was losing my motivation – and you just can't perform in this business without motivation!'

His relationship with Ron Dennis was deteriorating by this stage anyway. 'We had some terrible rows, no question about it,' says Barnard, 'and sometimes the situation became absolutely explosive. I could feel myself tensing up, mentally revving right off the scale. We went through some frightful times, but then it would calm down and be OK.' Unquestionably, Barnard was ripe for a change and, when it came, he was more than receptive. However, he stuck firmly to his guns that he was not, under any circumstances, going to leave his home in England. Ferrari, anxious to have his services at virtually any cost, agreed. Thus GTO came into being and John continued to work a short drive from his home.

Arriving at GTO, Barnard found that the new Ferrari F187 was in a pretty advanced stage of design when he inherited the project. 'I would have liked to change one or two details at the front end of the monocoque, but I was only able to change things like the top of the fuel cell,' he recalls. 'However, I did lay out the suspension geometry, waisted in the rear bodywork and added the aerodynamic ramps at the rear end. In addition, I gave Ferrari some fundamental requirements for a new longitudinal gearbox which went with their new 90-degree V6 engine. The only thing I really did on the engine front was to get the block torsion tested and, as a result, slightly stiffened.'

However, while Harvey Postlethwaite got on with the job of running the F187s in the field for much of the year, after the first few races Barnard spent as much time as possible back at GTO working on the new '3.5'. His arrival in the Maranello fold blew a new wind through the corridors of power – and a chill one, at that, in the opinion of many of his colleagues.

Barnard shook up the system, imposing a strict discipline on the way in which the team operated. Lambrusco with lunch at the races, or even test sessions, was out as far as the mechanics were concerned, he decreed. Barnard, the perfectionist, reckoned it was all going to be done *his* way. Michele Alboreto was also annoyed by the way in which John imposed his ideas on the team. For a while, it looked as though an ugly confrontation was brewing, but Ferrari pasted over the cracks. The perfectionist from McLaren looked like making life uncomfortable for quite a few people.

Barnard, however, made no apologies. 'Take a logical view,' he explained with his customary directness. 'I've been recruited to this position because Ferrari wants to improve its performance. I'm the bloke who's got to take the blame if it all goes wrong. So, the way I figure it, I'll be an idiot to myself if I don't get it done my way. If I can't have a free hand, then nobody should complain if the project doesn't work.'

Uncompromising and single-minded: those are the two adjectives that best describe John Barnard and his approach to F1 car design. Looking at the McLaren–TAG record, who's to argue against him?

Rory Byrne

Rory Byrne's commitment to the same team is on a par with Patrick Head's loyalty to Williams. For ten years he has worked for what started out as Toleman and later evolved into the Benetton organisation. Although his cars have so far only won a single Grand Prix, he enjoys a reputation as one of the more innovative designers in the F1 field.

Born in Pretoria, South Africa, on 10 January 1944, Rory's youthful preoccupation was with model gliders, his interest in and keen grasp of aerodynamics helping him to build the machine which won the World Hand Launched Gliding Championships in 1960, '61 and '63!

Graduating from Johannesburg's University of Witwatersrand with a B.Sc. in Industrial Chemistry, Rory got a job in his chosen field with Colchem during which time he began working on a Ford Anglia owned by a local saloon racer by the name of Barry Flowers. It was clear from pretty early on that Byrne's ambitions hardly lay in the area of industrial chemistry and, almost inevitably, he soon left Colchem to open a motor accessory

business at Alberton, south of Johannesburg. He also met up with Roy Klomfass and designed the Formula Ford Fulmen which Klomfass used to finish second in the 1972 South African FF series.

Although series champion Richard Sterne decided against taking the chance of continuing to race in Europe, Rory and Roy both decided that was the place to be in order to consolidate their racing futures. They arrived in the UK at the start of 1973, making a bee-line for Royale where Rory spent the season working on the Klomfass RP16. At the end of the year Chief Designer Bob King left the company owing to ill-health, leaving Alan Cornock with the responsibility of running the organisation. Cornock asked Byrne if he would take the post of designer; Rory accepted and took his first steps down the long road towards Formula 1.

Byrne's Royale designs proved to be prolific winners from the word go. They included the RP19 Super Vee, which won championships on both sides of the Atlantic, and the very successful RP21, which Geoff Lees used to win all the major British FF titles in 1975. But it was through an RP21 customer that Rory's big chance arose.

That customer was none other than Toleman Managing Director Alex Hawkridge. Their paths began to converge and, when the Byrne-designed RP25 was driven with such distinction by Rad Dougall, a link was unobtrusively established which would eventually lead to both Rad and Rory joining the Toleman F2 team (then based at Kidlington, near Oxford) in 1978. Rory was put in charge of the development of the March 782s, but at the end of the season he advised that they should switch to Ralts for 1979. It proved to be absolutely the right move, Brian Henton coming within a gnat's whisker of the '79 European F2 championship before winning it decisively in 1980 at the wheel of Rory's first Toleman design, the TG280.

Rory and his colleagues worked well with both engine builder Brian Hart, whose four-cylinder 420R F2 engine had propelled the TG280, and Pirelli, whose radial tyres the team had used and indeed would keep using on Toleman's graduation into F1 at the start of 1981. This was a massively ambitious project, involving a team new to F1, with a new engine, chassis and tyres, but they tackled the seemingly impossible with no more than a few fleeting misgivings.

Byrne's first machine, the TG181, was a compromise design simply to get the team on the road. Turbo installations, intercooler positions – they all represented totally new areas of technology for the Toleman lads, but Byrne didn't flinch. He pressed on in determined fashion. There were those who wondered why the team didn't kick off with a nice tried and trusted Cosworth DFV – 'just to get into the swing of things' – but Rory knew how inadvisable that would have been. 'We were committed to F1 with the Hart turbo from the outset,' he insisted, 'so there was no point messing around with some interim arrangement. It would not have made any sense. We had to jump in at the deep end and try to make the project work.'

In 1982 the revamped TG181B showed moderately promising form in several races, notably the British Grand Prix at Brands Hatch where Derek Warwick got ahead of Didier Pironi's Ferrari to hold second place behind Niki Lauda's McLaren. The car eventually stopped out on the circuit, allegedly with a broken driveshaft joint. Many people believe it ran short of fuel, racing deliberately with less than the team knew it would need to finish, in order to show well on the television at home . . .

Having come to grips with the challenges of turbo engine installation, Rory's next project was the neat, ground-effect TG183 intended to carry the team forward into 1983. Alas, a few weeks after its unveiling in September 1982, FISA banned sculptured aerodynamic underbodies, insisting on the flat-bottom rule as from the start of the following year. Byrne was obliged to revamp the car extensively to conform with the new rules, but it still showed considerable promise to give the team its first Championship points at the end of the season.

For 1984 Byrne had the treat of working with rising star Ayrton Senna, the Brazilian demonstrating considerable brilliance behind the wheel of the sleek TG184, taking second place at Monaco and rounding off the year with a strong third in Portugal, chasing the invincible McLaren–TAGs across the finishing line.

Rory's new TG185 looked as though it would be an outstanding contender in the hands of Stefan Johansson, but as things turned out, Toleman was destined for change. Owing to tyre supply problems, Byrne found himself and the team 'all dressed up with nowhere to go'. Goodyear was unable to assist when it came to supplying tyres, so they were now left out in the cold following their mid-season switch from Pirelli to Michelin and the subsequent withdrawal of the French concern from F1.

Only after buying out the Spirit team's tyre supply contract could Toleman go racing, now carrying the United Colors of Benetton livery. Rory's TG185 followed the usual Toleman form: promising, but never quite capable of producing the hard results. That all changed at the end of the year, however, when Benetton bought control of Toleman Group Motorsport, continuing to operate from the same Witney factory but swapping to BMW power. Teo Fabi stayed on the driving strength, now partnered by Austrian rising star Gerhard Berger. The true quality of Rory's machines would soon go on very public display.

When Berger's Pirelli-shod Benetton–BMW won the Mexican Grand Prix, it was a long overdue success for Byrne, the practical South African-born designer whose aerodynamic trademark had long been admired by his rivals. In fact, aerodynamic ingenuity and clever packaging are probably the two most outstanding features of the recent clutch of F1 machines spawned by Rory Byrne's efforts.

It is probably also fair to assume that Rory's Toleman/Benetton line would have won more races if he hadn't been faced with the time-consuming challenge of building chassis for four different engines in as many years. In quick succession, the team has moved from Hart (1985) to BMW (1986) to Ford turbo (1987) to Ford DFR (1988), never allowing itself the luxury of capitalising on an established format, honing a competitive concept into a second year. 'That has been pretty challenging and kept us *very* busy,' Byrne says, 'but it's taught everybody a great deal and I'm certain we have as big a bank of accumulated expertise as most current F1 teams, even if we are significantly younger than many of them!'

One of Colin Chapman's philosophical maxims used to be 'You give me a nice reliable 450 bhp V8 and I'll produce a chassis package which it will push through the air faster than a 525 bhp flat-12.' That was a dig at Ferrari, made at the time that his ground-effect Lotus 78 ruled the roost. A year or

Gerhard Berger scored the first victory for a Byrne-designed F1 machine when his Benetton–BMW won at Mexico City in 1986.

so later, Chapman offered Rory Byrne a job on the Hethel design staff. Rory declined, preferring to concentrate on his existing F2 project. But it was nice to have been asked.

Then, at the pre-season Rio test in 1987, the new Ford turbo-engined Benetton B187 was unveiled. In stark contrast to the previous year's Haas Lola, original recipient of the compact Ford V6 turbo, Byrne's new challenger featured a rear deck which hugged every contour of the low-slung V6. It was so low, it almost seemed difficult to believe there was an engine in it at all!

'I would expect that car to win three races this year,' predicted Williams designer Patrick Head. The fact that a series of frustrating minor technical faults prevented it from even winning one is neither here nor there. The point is that Byrne attracted the praise of one of his arch-rivals, a man with a reputation for high standards. That acknowledgement from Head was another coat of veneer on the gloss of Rory Byrne's standing in the F1 community.

145

Gerard Ducarouge

There is something symbolically appropriate about Gerard Ducarouge's role as Chief Engineer at Team Lotus. In 1981, after five years in charge of the design side at Ligier, 'Duca' was fired by the autocratic and unpredictable Guy – and Colin Chapman tried to recruit him to his Hethel-based team. Unfortunately, by that time Gerard already had an Alfa Romeo contract in his pocket. He stayed there until a major row in the summer of '83 drove him out of the Italian team's highly political environment. By then he was ready to come to Lotus, to *fill* Chapman's role rather than supplement it. Colin had been dead for eight months, his team struggling. Ducarouge was the catalyst required to put Lotus back on the road to the top . . .

Now one of the most widely respected engineer/designers in the business, Gerard's background was originally with the aerospace industry. After gaining an engineering degree, in the early 1960s he went to work for Nord Aviation on its missile programme, but being confined to the test centre near Paris was not Ducarouge's ideal. 'I'm a restless sort of person who doesn't always like to be in the same place,' he admits. 'I like to travel a lot and was looking forward to being assigned a post out on the company's missile testing ranges in South America. After a year with Nord Aviation there seemed little prospect of such an opportunity arising, so I was extremely disappointed about the way in which things seemed to be working out.'

Then, in December 1965, an advertisement caught his eye for a job as technician in the racing department of the fledgling Matra concern. It was at the time when Matra Sport was just starting to gain a reputation for building promising F3 cars and, with an F2 and sports car programme beckoning, Ducarouge took the job like a shot. He proved ideally suited for the demanding tasks ahead, staying with Matra right through to its withdrawal from the sports car racing arena at the end of 1974.

Gerard's time with Matra was spent exclusively on the team's sports car programmes, his more than passable English marking him out as the ideal liaison man between the French team and BRM, whose 2-litre engines were initially used to power Matra's Le Mans cars. He had nothing to do with the team's V12-engined F1 car, perhaps strangely, but writ his name large on the international endurance racing scene by masterminding Matra's hat-trick of Le Mans victories in 1972-74. Then Matra quit, sports car champions for the second straight year, and Gerard was faced with a choice.

'After all that fun with the racing programme, I could either opt for a job

Ducarouge forged a productive partnership with Mario Andretti during the second half of 1981.

146

within Matra's space division or accept an offer from Guy Ligier, who was taking the ambitious step up into F1 with his own car,' Gerard reflects. 'I had really loved my time in endurance racing; the reliance on a complete team effort, right through to the end of each event. You don't feel quite so involved as you do in F1. However, although Matra always did things in tremendous style, never compromising any of their technical efforts on grounds of expense, I was still only a relatively small fish in a big pond. With Ligier, I was being offered the opportunity to take charge of the whole technical side of the team's efforts.'

For the first three seasons Ligier's cars relied on Matra V12 engines, scoring only one victory in that time, but at the start of 1979 the team switched to Cosworth DFV power. More importantly, Gerard's knowledge of aerodynamics helped him design the superb JS11 chassis which, quite simply, brained the ground-effect opposition in the first two races of the year. They later won a third race, but subsequently their performances rather tailed off for a variety of unrelated reasons. However, Gerard recalls the JS11 as 'my most satisfying project up to that point in my career'.

A careful analysis of Team Lotus's efforts to date in the ground-effect arena enabled Ducarouge and his colleagues to produce a second-generation ground-effect machine which eclipsed the famous Lotus 79s at a stroke. What the French engineer had recognised before his rivals was the necessity to build a chassis stiff enough to sustain the increased downloads involved. However, Ligier was short of money, and the opposition cottoned on to what they were doing – and caught up. The initial Ducarouge advantage was squandered.

For 1981, Ligier switched back to Matra V12 power, as Talbot was now backing the team's efforts. The car went quite well but, immediately after the British GP at Silverstone, Guy Ligier fired his old colleague and collaborator with zero notice. 'Looking back on that moment over all these years, I am *still* not sure why he did that,' says Gerard quizzically. 'It was a bolt from the blue, I was absolutely stunned. It left many unanswered questions, but I can only assume that it had something to do with the fact that Jean-Pierre Jabouille had just joined the team. He was Laffite's brother-in-law, of course, and perhaps he had different ideas on the development routes we should be taking. But, really, I never quite got to the bottom of it all.'

Not that Ducarouge was unemployed for long. The Autodelta Alfa Romeo outfit quickly snapped him up to sort out their semi-works F1 effort. He quickly gained the faith of drivers Bruno Giacomelli and Mario Andretti, even if the latter was initially extremely suspicious of the Frenchman's rather sharp dress sense and immaculate hairstyles. By the end of the season, though, Mario conceded that Ducarouge worked more like Colin Chapman than any other engineer he had ever encountered.

Sadly, Gerard's talent was squandered at Alfa Romeo too. Basically he was a bit too good for the established 'old guard' in and around the Italian F1 team. Throughout 1982 he made progress with the Italian cars, de Cesaris taking pole at Long Beach in one of the 'Dook's' machines only to pile it into a wall during the race. Ducarouge spent a year sorting out Autodelta's operations, establishing a worthwhile and well-organised base – only for Alfa Romeo's President to come to him at the end of the season and tell him that plans were changing for 1983. Duca's new base would

148

The Frenchman celebrates Senna's victory with the Lotus 98T at Detroit, 1986.

never be used. Instead, the Alfa F1 effort was being farmed out to Paolo Pavanello's Euroracing organisation, a team hitherto experienced only in operating F3 machinery.

For Gerard, it was something of a nightmare. He talked in terms of expanding the team's R&D capacity, of building their own wind tunnel. By contrast, Pavanello seemed only interested in penny-pinching economies. The two men had a philosophical difference of approach. 'I soon realised that there was no way in which we could be really competitive under such a regime,' Ducarouge admits. 'There was no chance of winning races with such basic shortcomings.'

Eventually, internal politics would intervene to engineer his dismissal from the Alfa organisation, just as they had at Ligier. At the 1983 French Grand Prix, held on an untypically early date in April, de Cesaris's Alfa was found to have an empty on-board fire extinguisher bottle. The Italian was excluded after setting fastest time in the session during which he was running light with the empty bottle. Gerard carried the can and found himself dismissed. It was an amazingly short-sighted step for the Alfa outfit to take: events would subsequently prove they needed him more than he did them!

Up to this point Gerard had always felt nervous about joining Lotus, despite a generous offer from Chapman the previous summer. 'I was flown to Ketteringham Hall and just couldn't believe what I saw,' he said several years later. 'I had been accustomed to an industrial environment with Matra, Ligier and Alfa Romeo, so it came as a bit of a shock to find these elegant rural surroundings. But I found myself unable to accept the post. I was worried that I would find it difficult to work with such a genius, a man who had such a dominant personality. I have the same reservations about working for Ferrari. But I was proud and flattered to have been asked.'

Only after Chapman's death did Ducarouge feel comfortable about coming to Hethel to oversee what was, initially, a crash development programme on a new chassis to take the turbo Renault engine. The ungainly 93T had turned out to be an unwieldy truck, reflecting just how off-the-pace Lotus's design technology had drifted in the previous couple of seasons. In five weeks, Ducarouge pushed through the build programme to produce a brace of brand new 94Ts in time for the British Grand Prix at Silverstone.

Nigel Mansell drove brilliantly to take fourth place on the new car's maiden outing and, from that moment onwards, Lotus was back on the road to success.

Throughout the remainder of 1983 and the whole of '84, the Ducarouge Lotus–Renaults would prove highly competitive propositions. But for the arrival of the Michelin-shod McLaren–TAGs onto the scene in '84, Team Lotus would have returned to the winner's circle. Eventually, in 1985, the arrival of the gifted Ayrton Senna restored Hethel to its winning ways and, in '85 and '86, Gerard's Renault-engined designs were consistent front-runners. The team's fortunes dipped slightly in 1987, the Honda turbo-engined car proving no match for Patrick Head's Williams FW11B, even with Senna at the wheel, but they still won two Grands Prix despite this.

Ducarouge could not be described as a 'hands-on' designer in the sense that he works at a drawing board from dawn to dusk. Far from it. He is a concept man, clear-sighted and imbued with a wealth of knowledge of what's practical and what isn't. He is particularly adept at coaxing a design concept out of the drawing office staff at Ketteringham Hall. He will readily take advice from those who are more experienced in any specific area of Grand Prix car design, but his talent for producing a rounded, homogenous end product is his great strength. As a visualiser and an inspiration to his colleagues, he has a talent of which Colin Chapman would have been proud.

Colin Chapman, the genius into whose shoes Ducarouge stepped in the summer of 1983.

Patrick Head

When Patrick Head first met up with Frank Williams, towards the end of 1975, he wasn't quite sure what to make of him. At his interview for the post of engineer with Frank's beleaguered F1 team, which was on the verge of being swallowed up by Austro-Canadian oil millionaire, Walter Wolf, he was asked by Williams whether he was sufficiently committed to work twelve hours a day, seven days a week. Patrick replied that he wouldn't, 'because anybody who had to do that must be extremely badly organised'.

Head got the job, whether or not the answer he had given was regarded as the right one. The son of Colonel Michael Head, one-time military attaché to the British Embassy in Stockholm and a keen amateur racer, with a succession of Jaguar-engined sports cars in the 1950s, Patrick's enthusiasm for motor racing had started after his father's retirement from the cockpit in 1958. However, initially it looked as though his career path would lead him in another direction; after leaving Wellington College, he entered the Royal Naval College at Dartmouth, only to find within a very short space of time that he had made a major error of judgement. A few months later he bought himself out of the navy – a complicated and not inexpensive procedure.

There followed a rather fragmented and convoluted continuation of his education, culminating in his qualifying with a degree in engineering from University College, London. He then went off to work for Lola cars at Huntingdon, joining such aspiring colleagues as future McLaren–TAG designer, John Barnard. After what he regarded as a very worthwhile spell with this production racing car manufacturer Patrick moved on, to involve himself in a Formula Super Vee engine development project, working with preparation specialist Geoff Richardson, before the whole programme came to an unexpectedly premature end after Richardson's premises were gutted by fire. It was a case of 'on to the next item'...

After designing a neat little F2 car for Richard Scott to drive, Patrick moved about the motor racing business for the next two or three years, helping out at Trojan, with Ronnie Grant in Super Vee and Guy Edwards in F5000. Then came the meeting with Frank Williams at a London hotel, followed by the offer of a job. Of course, Walter Wolf did take control in 1976, so Patrick's design talents were cast in a supporting role to those of Harvey Postlethwaite. It was a catastrophic season, the Wolf–Williams FW05s (developed from the Hesketh 308C) turning out to be basically dreadful cars with virtually no good points. Patrick doesn't like to dwell on those

ungainly machines, but concedes that he learnt a lot. 'More about what not to do than anything else,' he grins. The experience stood him in good stead for the future.

By the end of 1976, Frank Williams couldn't stand his role as highly paid ADC to Walter Wolf any longer. He wanted to be in 'hands-on' control of a racing team, and it had become increasingly obvious that he would be allowed no such luxury in the Wolf set-up. He took the decision to start up on his own, running a private March 771 for Belgian Patrick Neve, and asked Head whether he would come and engineer the car. Patrick did so but, more importantly, he also began laying the technical groundwork for future success. Frank Williams was courting the Saudis for sponsorship and, throughout the long summer of '77, Head toiled away at the team's new Didcot base, producing the compact F1 design which would start putting Williams seriously on the map – the FW06.

Patrick's first complete F1 design was, in some ways, a 'seat-of-the-pants' affair. There was insufficient finance to utilise a wind tunnel and, being a fundamentally conservative engineer, Patrick shied away from trying to imitate the Lotus wing-car concept, confessing that he 'frankly didn't understand how it worked'. Accordingly, he built a conventional and ultra-compact flat-bottomed machine. Alan Jones was signed to drive and the team was on its way.

Almost from the start of the season, the FW06 ran strongly. It was a practical, easy-to-service and operate machine, in many ways sharing the no-nonsense approach of its sometimes rather bellicose designer. It only took a few races for Frank and Patrick to realise that they had recruited a kindred spirit in their new driver. Down-to-earth and straightforward, with no hang-ups, Alan Jones just wanted to get the job done.

Not that 1978 was straightforward, by any stretch of the imagination, but Patrick found Jones's stoicism a great help to a designer in times of trouble. During practice for the US Grand Prix at Watkins Glen, Alan crashed heavily following a breakage of a wheel-retaining through-bolt, a failure which, he admits, made him feel sick to his stomach. Thankfully a local firm was found who, somewhat reluctantly, agreed to re-heat-treat some replacement through-bolts overnight and Jones was able to compete in the race after all, speeding to a superb second place behind Carlos Reutemann's Ferrari T3.

Patrick couldn't look. He stood in the pits, not daring to watch as Jones went about his business in FW06. Just two years later, Patrick would stand in the Montreal pit lane in a similar state of nerves, again not daring to look. But this time Jones would be out on the circuit in the FW07B, storming to the victory which would clinch him the 1980 World Championship. Head might not have known much about ground-effect in 1978, but by 1979 he had produced the Williams FW07. It was the car which would set fresh standards in the evolution of ground-effect F1 cars, as well as being the machine which finally put the team on the map, Clay Regazzoni scoring the Williams marque's first win in the 1979 British Grand Prix.

From that point onwards, Head came to be acknowledged as one of the most accomplished designers in the business and the FW07 series remained one of F1's pacemakers right through until its replacement by the FW08 at the start of the 1982 European season. By this point the original triumvirate had broken up, Alan Jones retiring from the cockpit (albeit temporarily) following

a superb flag-to-flag victory in the inaugural Las Vegas Grand Prix. His place in the team was taken by the rugged Keke Rosberg, who once remarked later, 'I don't think that Frank and Patrick ever quite forgave me for not being Alan Jones.' It was a typical Keke remark – acid, sly and perceptive – but most people in F1 knew precisely what he meant. It never was quite the same. . .

For Patrick, of course, there was fresh technical ground to conquer. First, 1983 saw the necessity to rejig the FW08 to conform to the new flat-bottomed technical regulations but also, and more important in the long term, Williams struck a deal with Honda for the supply of turbocharged F1 engines. This involved Patrick in the task of producing the first prototype FW09 by the end of '83, for a planned debut at Kyalami in the last race of the season. It wasn't just a question of building a totally new car, but a matter of evolving a new engine installation, working out profiles of exhaust pipes, water radiators and turbo intercoolers. 'It was a challenge. The engine just arrived in a box with nothing attached,' he reflects. 'They just didn't have any accumulated data to draw on. OK, they'd done a year with the Spirit operation, but that didn't amount to much. In effect, they came to us as novices in the F1 game.'

It is recent history how Patrick Head's design team built a succession of Honda-engined F1 cars which progressively improved to the point where they won the 1986 and '87 World Constructors' Championship, establishing themselves as the car to beat throughout both seasons. However, at the end of 1987, the team's failure to secure Nelson Piquet the Drivers' World Championship in the first of those years led to Honda taking its engines elsewhere – to McLaren. Head found himself back designing a naturally aspirated Grand Prix car for 1988, using the 3.5-litre V8 engine produced by Rugby engine specialist John Judd, another straightforward and practical engineer in the same mould as the Williams Chief Designer.

'I suppose from the engineering point of view, it's great to win the Constructors' Championship,' reflects Patrick, 'but the fact of the matter is that while everybody knows who won the Drivers' Championship, only a handful can recall the Champion constructor from any specific season off the top of their heads. For that reason, you have to say that even a designer would really like to win a Drivers' title, rather than one for the Constructors.'

Patrick Head at his office desk in the Williams team's Didcot headquarters.

Gordon Murray

Now Technical Director of McLaren International, Gordon Murray's name seemed inseparably linked with the fortunes of Bernie Ecclestone's Brabham team for more than a decade. This calm, artistic and ambitious South African-born designer was responsible for F1 Brabhams from 1973 through until the end of 1986 when the partnership finally split up after their joint fortunes plumbed fresh depths of disappointment with the unsuccessful, striking low-line BT55.

However, Gordon's knowledge of the technical organisation required to build World Championship-winning Grand Prix cars was just what Ron Dennis was looking for when it came to replacing John Barnard within the McLaren team's structure. Barnard had established himself as an all-dominant, supremely powerful figure within McLaren and Dennis didn't want this situation repeating itself. Murray's task was to preside over a department which would involve more input from a wider variety of sources. John's mercurial talent had a temper to go with it, but Gordon brought a quieter, more placid mood to the McLaren design department.

Born in Durban in 1946, Gordon took a part-time course in engineering at Natal Technical College for five years from the age of 18, at the same time working as a mechanical design draughtsman. His father Bill raced motor cycles and later prepared racing cars for local Durban driver Gordon Henderson, this paternal enthusiasm rubbing off on young Murray. He was barely 20 when he built his own Lotus 7-style sports car to race in club events and hillclimbs, its engine based on a reworked Ford Anglia 105E unit. The whole project showed that Gordon had a tremendous amount of technical initiative although, as he said: 'You couldn't really buy any decent cars out there at the time, so if you wanted something fast, then you had to build it yourself.'

In December 1969 Gordon set off for England, not quite knowing what he was going to do – or what sort of weather he could be expected to encounter on his arrival. He'd written to the Director of Vehicle Engineering at Lotus Cars, inquiring about the possibility of a job on the road car side, but the famous Norfolk-based car company were going through a bad patch, laying workers off, so there was no chance there. Funnily enough, although he was an ardent fan of Colin Chapman, he didn't give a thought to applying for a job with the racing team. He didn't think he had the necessary experience. As an aside, he also arrived in the middle of winter without so much as a pullover –

157

'I just don't know what I could have been thinking about' – and his inexperience showed in other ways, too. 'I went up to see Lotus by *coach*, would you believe, thinking that they were the quickest means of travel, as they were in South Africa. I didn't think of catching a train...'

Eventually he had a lucky break, walking into the Brabham workshops at New Haw, near Weybridge, on the off-chance, only to be mistaken for a formal applicant for a job. Ron Tauranac hired him, he feels, 'on the basis that I'd demonstrated some practical mechanical ability in designing and building my own car. There were others who had better engineering qualifications, but I reckon that Ron gave me the job because I'd done something like that off my own back.'

Gordon spent 1970 doing minor detail design work on wishbones and roll-over bars, eventually deciding that perhaps he wasn't so keen to stay on under Ron's regime, accepting instead an offer to design the Duckhams sports car for Alain de Cadenet and Chris Craft to race at Le Mans. 'Then I heard that Bernie Ecclestone was about to take over the company, so I hung on, thinking things would get better.' However, he was still fully committed to the Duckhams, so spent much of the year working 20-hour days – going home at ten o'clock from the Brabham factory, working on the Duckhams design until three in the morning and then up again at seven o'clock to get back to the Brabham base an hour later. 'That nonsense went on for three months until I got the Le Mans car ready!'

Throughout 1972 Gordon effectively acted as Ralph Bellamy's understudy and, at the end of the year, received an offer to join Tecno to help on the flat-12 F1 project. A lot of money was on the table but, mercifully, Murray resisted a proposition which might well have finished his F1 design career there and then. Meanwhile, back at base, Bellamy accepted an offer from Lotus, so Bernie called Gordon into his office and told him he had a clean sheet of paper to design a totally new F1 Brabham for 1973. 'He didn't want me to use any of the old components. I had a free hand, so I decided to stay on!'

The first of the new-breed Brabhams was the pyramid monocoque BT42, germinating from an original concept kicked about by Gordon and Bellamy the previous season. 'I was also doing the job of factory manager and storeman as well,' he recalls, 'so life was pretty hectic.' The first BT42 was written off by John Watson in the Race of Champions, but a replacement was ready in time for Carlos Reutemann to use at Barcelona where only the failure of a rubber boot on a driveshaft constant velocity joint prevented him challenging for the lead.

The BT42 was acknowledged as a promising machine, but Murray really established himself in the forefront of contemporary design technology with its successor, the BT44. With its inboard front suspension activated by pullrods, the car was lighter, tidier and more compact than before. Reutemann dominated his home Grand Prix at Buenos Aires before running out of fuel near the finish. The car then went on to win three GPs in the hands of the brilliant Argentinian driver – South Africa, Austria and the US event. Murray further refined this concept for '75, the BT44Bs winning in Brazil (Carlos Pace) and Germany (Reutemann). Gordon had made his name, but a bigger challenge awaited him in 1976.

Ecclestone did a deal for the supply of Alfa Romeo engines, posing

The distinctive 'pyramid' monocoque Brabham BT44B on its way to victory in the 1975 Brazilian Grand Prix in the hands of the late Carlos Pace.

Gordon the challenge of producing a totally new car from the ground up to accommodate the bulky, thirsty flat-12 Alfa Romeo engine. 'I had to abandon our pyramid monocoque layout,' he explained, 'because we were faced with the problem of packaging a much bigger fuel load than we had to cater for with the Cosworth car.' The BT46s were heavy and unwieldy to start with, but gradually Murray honed them into highly competitive propositions. By the middle of 1977 they were running regularly at the front of the field, yet a succession of minor technical snags prevented them from nailing that elusive first victory.

For 1978, Niki Lauda was signed up by Ecclestone, the twice World Champion switching from Ferrari. Bernie's salesmanship was sufficiently persuasive for him to clinch the deal by showing the Austrian driver Gordon's latest baby, the prototype 'surface cooled' BT46. As it turned out, the surface cooling system proved a complete non-starter, leaving Murray to revamp the car and, eventually, to come up with the 'fan car' concept which was withdrawn, amidst a hail of protest from his rivals, after Niki sped to an easy victory in the Swedish Grand Prix.

For 1979, Murray told Alfa that they would have to build a V12 engine to enable Brabham to produce a proper ground-effect car and, without turning a hair, the Italian firm did just that. 'I was amazed at the briskly efficient way they just got on and did it,' says Gordon with admiration. 'I just couldn't believe how quickly they moved.' The striking new BT48 was rolled out just before Christmas 1978, but proved less than totally competitive once the '79 season got underway. However, a switch back to Ford–Cosworth DFV power in the late summer was too late to prevent a disillusioned Lauda from quitting the cockpit midway through practice for the Canadian Grand Prix.

Murray with McLaren boss Ron Dennis. Gordon joined McLaren from Brabham at the start of 1987.

For two more seasons, Murray's neat and compact BT49 derivatives represented the team's fortunes, until Bernie brought them into the turbo era by forging a deal with BMW. All Gordon's cars gained a reputation for attention to detail and a high standard of finish, and when Nelson Piquet clinched the '81 World Championship with a fifth-place finish at Las Vegas, it was the first title success for the team since Denny Hulme became World Champion with Repco power back in 1967. Nelson stayed on with Brabham through to the end of 1984, winning another title with BMW power in '83. He forged an understanding and sympathetic relationship with Gordon Murray who reckoned Piquet 'was one of the very best test and development drivers I ever worked with. He was supremely intelligent and, learning a lot from Niki Lauda, quickly worked out how to sift through the input he was gathering from the car to decide which items were relevant and which were not. In that respect, he was quite outstanding.'

Inevitably, though, there were always critics from rival teams who pointed accusing fingers at Gordon, accusing him of getting prior knowledge of rule changes because he worked for the man who was also President of the Formula One Constructors' Association. 'In fact that wasn't the case at all,' Gordon insists, pointing out that the team had built the first ground-effect half-tank BT51 'pit stop' car in preparation for the 1983 season because Bernie was still convinced that ground-effect underbodies would be retained. 'When they were outlawed, we had to start completely from scratch with the BT52. It wasn't a situation which suggested that Bernie had prior knowledge, in fact it was quite the reverse.'

However, through 1984 and '85 the Brabham–BMWs had a lean time in F1 and, after Murray produced the low-line BT55 for the 1986 season, in many ways it was the last roll of the dice for his relationship with Bernie. Over the previous two seasons one could sense that the two men were no longer as close as they had been in the past; Bernie's willingness to let Piquet go to Williams because he wasn't prepared to pay more for the twice World Champion's services particularly irked his designer.

The relationship had run its course by the end of 1986, after which the genial, good-humoured Gordon departed to plough a new furrow at McLaren. In many ways it was the end of an era.

Harvey Postlethwaite

Harvey was one of the pivotal personalities who contributed to Ferrari's mid-1980s renaissance, his arrival at Maranello predating John Barnard's by almost five years. A year into its turbo-engine development, the Ferrari team quite rightly concluded in the summer of 1981 that it was getting left behind in terms of chassis technology, both from the point of view of constructional knowledge and track performance. Postlethwaite was the man they selected to help steer them back towards the competitive path.

At the time that Maranello beckoned, Harvey was Chief Designer of the financially strapped Fittipaldi team, acutely frustrated by lack of resources. He had been in F1 for the best part of eight years, first working for Lord Hesketh's extrovert F1 team and subsequently for Walter Wolf Racing, designing the car in which Jody Scheckter finished runner-up in the 1977 World Championship. Postlethwaite was used to better things than Fittipaldi could promise in '81, so when the Ferrari offer came he accepted with alacrity, moving his family to Italy without a moment's hesitation.

Harvey qualified from Birmingham University with a B.Sc. in mechanical engineering, after which he spent another three years taking a course which eventually led to a Ph.D. for investigative and original studies in the specialised field of automotive crash research. In 1968 and 1969 he dabbled briefly in minor-league club racing with a U2 clubmans car, but quickly reached the conclusion that he was rather more adept at designing racing cars than driving them in anger.

Like John Barnard, Harvey's first job after finishing his studies was outside the motor racing spectrum. He joined ICI's research and development department at Runcorn, in Cheshire, where he busied himself on a variety of prototype projects, one of which included a rubber foam carburettor. 'It worked reasonably well,' he recalls with an air of faint nostalgia, 'but the motor industry wasn't terribly interested…'

It did not take long for Harvey to conclude that the rather clinical environment in which he found himself was not really to his taste. When a friend drew his attention to an advertisement in the *Daily Telegraph* offering a post for a mechanical engineer at March's Bicester factory, he wrote off immediately. The response to that advertisement simply took Robin Herd's breath away: over 250 applications were received. But Harvey was the man who got the job.

His early March projects included the development of their 2-litre sports car and development work – with Niki Lauda – on the BMW-engined 732 in which Jean-Pierre Jarier won the 1973 European F2 Championship. Postlethwaite quickly gained a reputation as a straightforward and practical engineer, but his sights were set firmly on F1. When Lord Hesketh acquired a March 731 for James Hunt to drive at the start of '73, Harvey accepted the peer's invitation to join the ambitious young outfit, to preside over the technical side. It was here that Harvey really began making his mark and, by the end of the year, the Hesketh 731 had been developed to the point where it was in a different league from the works cars. Driving 'Harvey's March', Hunt finished the year on a high note with a strong second place to Ronnie Peterson's pace-setting Lotus 72 in the US GP at Watkins Glen.

Clearly a lot had been learned in Hesketh's pilot season, but there was no way in which the 731 would last out another year. For 1974 Harvey produced a totally new car, the compact Hesketh 308, derivatives of which James used for two seasons. He won the '74 Silverstone International Trophy non-title thrash and in 1975 defeated World Champion-elect Niki Lauda's Ferrari 312T to take the Dutch Grand Prix at Zandvoort after an epic chase.

By the end of '75 Harvey had pencilled the totally new, ambitious rubber-suspended Hesketh 308C, but when his lordship decided to quit, unable to raise the necessary commercial backing to keep the team afloat, the assets of the team were taken over by Canadian oil man Walter Wolf, nominally in conjunction with Frank Williams. There followed a disjointed, disastrous 1976 season during which Frank split to set up again on his own, while Wolf decided to regroup for '77, signing Jody Scheckter to drive in what started out as a one-car team and giving Harvey *carte blanche* to design a totally new car.

Harvey's first Wolf design was a classic case of the right car for the right moment. It was compact, straightforward and conventional for that last season before ground-effect technology really moved into top gear. Jody used it to win in Argentina, Monaco and Canada, getting to within spitting distance of Niki Lauda in the battle for the Championship.

Postlethwaite followed the ground-effect route for 1978 with the Wolf WR6, a car which showed great promise but was bugged by a succession of minor problems. The great days of Wolf racing soon passed, leaving Harvey with the task of designing the alloy honeycomb Wolf WR8 for James Hunt in 1979. James quit midway through the season, a decision which Harvey took very personally at the time, regarding it almost as a betrayal.

In 1980 the Wolf team's assets were taken over – along with the cars – by the Fittipaldi brothers, Emerson and Wilson, after which fortunes plummeted through to the early summer of 1981 when Harvey received that approach from Ferrari.

Harvey's knowledge of contemporary chassis design technique was just what Ferrari needed, so while Gilles Villeneuve and Didier Pironi wrestled the unwieldy 126CK along the World Championship trail, Postlethwaite set to work at the factory, first taking stock of the situation and then taking the most practical steps to bring Ferrari's chassis capability up to speed. 'To be frank, I think I would have really liked to produce a carbon-fibre composite chassis for the 1982 season,' he explained, 'but although I felt I had the necessary knowledge required to do it, I found Ferrari was really quite a long way behind some of its English rivals and, also, if we were going to tackle this new technology on our own, then we should be in a position to carry out all the manufacturing processes in-house. So, for 1982, we adopted a two-pronged attack: we began to get ourselves organised on the carbon composite front while I built an alloy honeycomb chassis for the team to race in 1982.'

The result was, of course, the 126C2, to be followed 18 months later by the carbon-fibre composite C3. In his usual unobtrusively efficient manner, Harvey put in an enormous amount of work during those two seasons and certainly played a major role in reversing Ferrari's decline. As a measure of his success, it should be remembered that the C2 and C3 triumphed in the 1982-83 Constructors' Championship, a fact often overlooked by historians who readily recall Rosberg and Piquet taking the Drivers' titles.

'Of course, the accidents to Gilles Villeneuve and Didier Pironi really

took the glitter off those two seasons,' Harvey admits, 'and I must say, Gilles's fatal crash at Zolder really got to me. He was a great guy who gave absolutely everything he had to the business of driving racing cars to the absolute maximum of his potential. He was also one of the most disarmingly honest people I've ever met in racing. Take testing: he would spend a day flogging round Fiorano, pausing only to say "I don't mind driving round here all day in this car, but you ought to know that it's rubbish…" He was totally non-political with absolutely no hang-ups at all. Mr Ferrari loved him for this whole approach.

'His accident marked the first occasion on which any driver had been killed at the wheel of a car that I had designed, so I was obviously very concerned about the way in which Ferrari attracted so much criticism, calling into question the structural integrity of its cars. People said that the monocoque should not have broken up under impact in the way that it did, but we subsequently carried out static rig tests to destruction on one of the original 126CKs and a later C2, like the one Gilles was killed in, and I concluded that there was no question mark over the car's strength – and that few people in the F1 business actually had much understanding about the forces involved in such high speed accidents.'

Harvey remained at Maranello, having weathered the 1985-86 storm of discontent revolving round the team's lack of results. Between Michele Alboreto's victory in the 1985 German Grand Prix and Gerhard Berger's success in Japan, at the end of 1987, Ferrari had its longest-ever spell away from the winner's rostrum. The F186 used by Alboreto and Stefan Johansson was conspicuously unsuccessful, a failure due in part to Maranello lacking its own wind-tunnel facilities at a time when a more crucial premium than ever before was being placed on aerodynamic efficiency. By the end of 1986, a computer-monitored wind tunnel had been installed at the Ferrari racing headquarters, but by this stage it seemed to outsiders as though Harvey's position had been usurped by the arrival of John Barnard as Technical Director.

In fact, Harvey's amenable nature, Italian domicile and popularity among his peers ensured that he not only survived, but initially prospered under the new regime. The 1987 Ferrari F187 had originally been pencilled by Gustav Brunner before his departure from the team, Barnard adding some late modifications to the monocoque profile as well as outlining the finished car's general configuration, suspension geometry and aerodynamic detailing, such as the rear body waisting and rear ramps (his trademark from the McLaren days). But, say the drivers, it was Harvey's aerodynamic set-up which brought the car up to winning pace mid-season.

'We programme the computer and that tells us what set-up we need for which circuit and, as far as the drivers are concerned, the cars are adjusted to these settings almost before they are loaded into the transporter,' said Harvey with some satisfaction. 'Sometimes Gerhard will say "I think such-and-such would be better..." so we give him ten minutes to experiment, then get the programme back on course when he finds it is no improvement!'

Harvey Postlethwaite's standing with those in the corridors of power at Maranello rose considerably in 1987, but his fundamental popularity and commitment to the Ferrari cause were never in doubt from the day he first joined the team. His home was in a village near Maranello, where he, his wife Cherry and two children slipped into the relaxed Italian way of life. He even made his own version of that sparkling Lambrusco, but probably didn't tell John Barnard about that . . .

'The people at Ferrari have a great desire to do things properly,' Harvey insisted, 'and once you've shown them what might turn out to be a better way of doing something, then they'll try it. After you have worked with all these facilities and resources, it's a bit difficult to envisage going back to work with any other F1 team in this game!'

However, the political manoeuvrings behind the scenes at Maranello during the early summer of 1988 resulted in Harvey leaving the team and returning to England.

164

TECHNICAL OVERVIEW, 1977-88

In an attempt to encapsulate the dramatic technical development which occurred between the introduction of the first 'wing car' and the height of the turbo era, this section includes a potted specification of three significant cars from each of those twelve seasons. Additionally, a summary of the direction taken by F1 design trends during that year is included.

1977

Summary

Degree of technical conformity breached by Chapman's Lotus 78 which initiates the use of aerodynamic side pods, although cluttered outboard rear spring/ dampers still compromise overall concept. Contrasts with conventional approach still being adopted by Wolf – classic 'British standard kit car' of the time – and Ferrari, whose monocoque constructional techniques are essentially unchanged since 1970. However, Maranello's neat transverse gearbox, ahead of rear axle-line, a major factor contributing towards generally neutral, consistent handling qualities praised by T2's drivers.

Lotus 78–Ford/Cosworth

Chassis: sophisticated monocoque fuselage manufactured from Cellite sandwich material and aluminium panelling. Three fuel cells, in line across the car, positioned behind driver and extending into both side pods. Water radiators inset within leading edge of wing-profile aerodynamic side pods. Oil-cooler in nose.

Suspension: rocker arms activating inboard coil-spring/dampers at front; bottom wishbones, parallel top links, twin radius rods and outboard spring/dampers at rear.

Engine: Ford–Cosworth DFV installed as stressed member.

Transmission: Hewland FG400 five-speed proprietary unit.

Ferrari 312T2/77

Chassis: traditional multi-tube frame overlaid with semi-stressed panelling. Fuel tanks situated behind/alongside driver. 'Bathtub'-style construction with totally separate removable one-piece body top. Full length side pods incorporating water radiators/oil-coolers, but flat-bottom construction.

Suspension: double wishbones with inboard spring/dampers at the front; parallel links, single top link, twin radius rods and outboard spring/dampers at rear.

Engine: Ferrari 312 Boxer 180-degree 12-cylinder installed as stressed member.

Transmission: Ferrari transverse five-speed, mounted ahead of rear axle-line.

Wolf WR–Ford/Cosworth

Chassis: ultra-conventional, compact 'bathtub'-style monocoque manufactured from aluminium alloy sheeting with alloy bulkheads. Fuel tanks behind/alongside driver. Nose-mounted water radiator.

Suspension: double wishbones with outboard spring/dampers at front; parallel links, single top link, twin radius rods and outboard spring/dampers at rear.

Engine: Ford–Cosworth DFV installed as stressed member.

Transmission: Hewland FGA400 six-speed proprietary unit with detailed modifications to suit individual team.

1978

Summary

Chapman now really setting the pace with more refined ground-effect type 79, tidying up the type 78 concept to produce a tremendously competitive, effective package. Renault's first full year as turbo contenders sees them concentrate on uncomplicated, flat-bottomed chassis while developing turbo 1½-litre engine. Brabham's approach is over-complex, restricted by flat-12 engine which precludes any attempt at ground effect, apart from 'fan car' experiment which produces win in Sweden on sole outing, thereafter withdrawn.

Brabham BT46–Alfa Romeo

Chassis: high-sided, pyramidal aluminium alloy monocoque with rearward extending 'pontoons' to allow installation of flat-12 cylinder Alfa engine. Initial complex surface-cooling system abandoned, giving way to front-mounted radiators and later, briefly, 'fan car' concept.

Suspension: double wishbones with semi-inboard spring/dampers at front; single top link, parallel lower links and twin radius rods with outboard spring/dampers at rear.

Engine: Alfa Romeo 180-degree 12-cylinder mounted between rearward extensions of main monocoque.

Transmission: Brabham/Alfa Romeo casing, Hewland internals, five or six speeds.

Lotus 79–Ford/Cosworth

Chassis: slim central aluminium fuselage with stressed panelling arching over driver's legs. Single central fuel cell, side-mounted radiators. Full length ground-effect side pods, with sliding skirts.

Suspension: inboard spring/dampers activated by rocker arms front and rear, with lower wishbones.

Engine: Ford–Cosworth DFV installed as stressed member.

Transmission: Hewland FG400 five-speed proprietary unit. Lotus/Getrag experimental transmission also tested.

Renault RS01

Chassis: straightforward aluminium 'bathtub' monocoque, formed from two large alloy panels stiffened by internal steel strap plates. Nose-mounted oil-cooler, water radiators and intercoolers in side pods. Flat bottom to chassis.

Suspension: top rocker arms activating inboard spring/dampers at front; parallel lower links, single top link and twin radius rods with outboard spring/dampers at rear.

Engine: Renault EF1 1½-litre twin turbo V6.

Transmission: Hewland FGA400 six-speed proprietary unit.

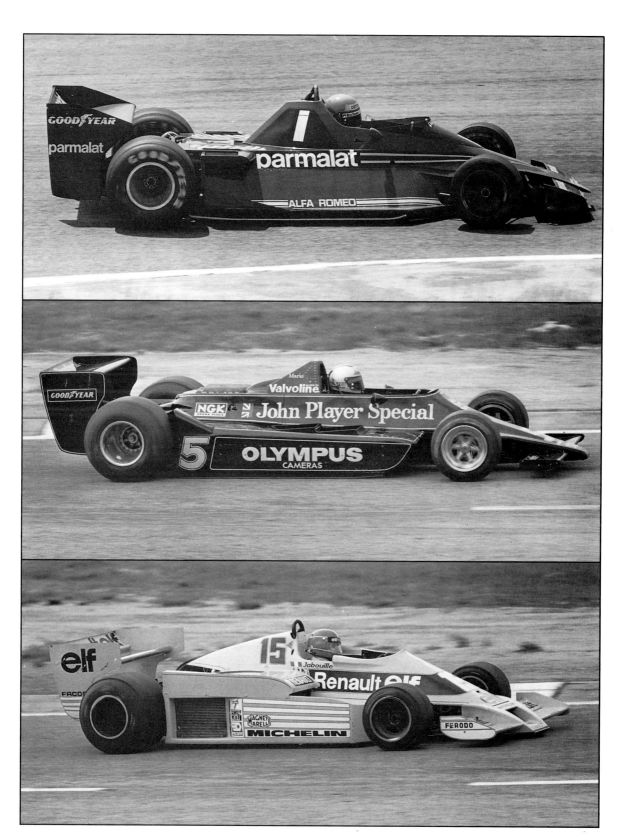

169

1979

Summary

Wide disparity of designs now, but crucial ground-effect aspect addressed by all three featured cars, although Ferrari hampered by too-wide flat-12 engine and Renault still at relatively early stage of turbo V6 development. Patrick Head's Williams design takes Chapman's ground-effect principles a stage further with appreciation of need for ultra-stiff structure to control ground-effect forces.

Ferrari 312T4

Chassis: latticework of small diameter tubes overlaid with aluminium panelling, similar to 1977 chassis. Bathtub monocoque, single fuel cell now behind driver. Sculptured aerodynamic side pods, but venturi size restricted by width of flat-12 cylinder engine. Radiator on left, oil-cooler on right.

Suspension: inboard spring/damper units all round, activated by rocker arms. Rear dampers running within special channels in casting behind rear axle-line.

Engine: Ferrari 312 Boxer 180-degree 12-cylinder installed as stressed member.

Transmission: Ferrari transverse five-speed, mounted ahead of rear axle-line.

Williams FW07–Ford/Cosworth

Chassis: slim monocoque manufactured from aluminium honeycomb material for additional torsional rigidity. Stressed panelling arched over driver's legs. Single fuel cell behind driver. Side-mounted radiators. Full length ground-effect side pods with sliding skirts.

Suspension: inboard spring/damper units front and rear activated by rocker arms with lower wishbones.

Engine: Ford–Cosworth DFV installed as stressed member.

Transmission: Hewland FGB gearbox modified by Williams with revised lubrication system.

Renault RS10

Chassis: aluminium alloy sheeting, now with stressed, curved panel over driver's legs. Top-louvred full length ground-effect side pods containing water radiators and intercoolers.

Suspension: inboard spring/damper units all round activated by rocker arms with lower wishbones.

Engine: Renault EF1 1½-litre twin turbo V6.

Transmission: Hewland FGA400 six-speed proprietary unit.

1980

Summary

Three typical DFV-engined cars, all to very similar general technical configuration, but note pullrod suspension activation and use of some carbon-fibre panels on the Brabham. On paper, one might believe that these cars were very similar, but the demands of ground-effect aerodynamics had by now become the key to success in this immediate pre-turbo era. The updated Williams FW07 (see notes on 1979) had now become the car to beat with the three cars featured offering a widely varying degree of challenge.

Ligier JS11/15–Ford/Cosworth

Chassis: aluminium alloy panelling. Fully enclosed over driver's feet. Ground-effect side pods incorporating water radiators and oil-coolers.

Suspension: inboard spring/damper units front and rear activated by rocker arms.

Engine: Ford–Cosworth DFV installed as stressed member.

Transmission: Hewland FGB five-speed proprietary unit.

Brabham BT49/49B–Ford/Cosworth

Chassis: aluminium honeycomb panelling with some non-stress-bearing areas in carbon-fibre panelling. Fully enclosed over driver's feet. Neat ground-effect side pods containing water radiators.

Suspension: double wishbones front and rear with semi-inboard spring/dampers activated by pullrods.

Engine: Ford–Cosworth DFV installed as stressed member.

Transmission: Brabham/Alfa casing, Hewland internals. Transverse Weismann unit also evaluated.

McLaren M29B/C–Ford/Cosworth

Chassis: aluminium alloy panelling. Fully enclosed over driver's feet. Ground-effect side pods incorporating water radiators and oil-coolers.

Suspension: inboard spring/damper units front and rear activated by rocker arms.

Engine: Ford–Cosworth DFV installed as stressed member.

Transmission: McLaren casing, Hewland internals, five speeds.

1981

Summary

Ferrari arrives in the turbo ranks, still using basic chassis-construction techniques from ten years before, clearly regarding engine as number one priority. Brabham BT50 a more sophisticated chassis/suspension package, while Alfa mark time with V12 waiting for turbo development. Rocker arm suspension still widely used, but many soon to follow pull/pushrod route.

Brabham BT50–BMW

Chassis: aluminium honeycomb with certain panels from carbon fibre. Ground-effect side pods incorporating radiators and intercoolers.

Suspension: semi-inboard spring/dampers front and rear with double wishbone set-up and pullrod activation.

Engine: BMW M12/13 1½-litre single turbo four cylinder.

Transmission: Brabham/Alfa Romeo casing, Hewland internals.

Ferrari 126C

Chassis: small diameter tubular frame overlaid with aluminium panelling. Ground-effect side pods rather crude, incorporating intercoolers and water radiators.

Suspension: inboard spring/dampers front and rear activated by rocker arms with lower wishbones.

Engine: Ferrari 120-degree 1½-litre twin turbo V6.

Transmission: Ferrari transverse five-speed, mounted ahead of rear axle-line.

Alfa Romeo 179

Chassis: aluminium alloy panelling. Ground-effect side pods housing water radiators and oil-coolers.

Suspension: inboard spring/dampers front and rear activated by rocker arms, and lower wishbones.

Engine: Alfa Romeo type 1260 3-litre V12.

Transmission: five-speed Alfa Romeo.

1982

Summary

Most significant move is the adoption by John Barnard of carbon-fibre monocoque for new McLaren MP4, presaging perhaps the most successful range of cars for a decade. Patrick Head's approach conservative, still retaining aluminium honeycomb construction while Ferrari at last makes move to similar chassis-manufacturing process. Williams adopt pullrod suspension, for aerodynamic reasons, and Ferrari follows mid-season on front of C2. McLaren runs to end of year with rocker-arm system. Constructional technology and attention to detail starting to become regular hallmark of front-running cars.

Williams FW08–Ford/Cosworth

Chassis: aluminium honeycomb monocoque, totally enclosed above driver's legs. Ground-effect side pods with fixed skirts housing water radiators and oil-coolers.

Suspension: upper and lower wishbones with inboard spring/dampers activated by pullrods at front; rocker arms activating inboard spring/dampers at rear with lower wishbones.

Engine: Ford–Cosworth DFV installed as stressed member.

Transmission: Williams casing, Hewland internals, five speeds.

Ferrari 126C2

Chassis: aluminium honeycomb monocoque, totally enclosed above driver's legs. Ground-effect side pods with fixed skirts housing turbo intercoolers, oil and water radiators.

Suspension: rocker arms activating inboard spring/dampers front and rear with lower wishbones. Later upper and lower wishbones with pullrod activation of spring/damper on front only.

Engine: Ferrari 120-degree 1½-litre twin turbo V6.

Transmission: Ferrari transverse five-speed, mounted ahead of rear axle-line.

McLaren MP4–Ford/Cosworth

Chassis: monocoque manufactured from carbon-fibre composite panels, totally enclosed above driver's legs. Ground-effect side pods with fixed skirts housing water and oil radiators.

Suspension: rocker arms activating inboard spring/damper units front and rear with lower wishbones.

Engine: Ford–Cosworth DFV installed as stressed member.

Transmission: McLaren casing, Hewland internals, five speeds.

1983

Summary

The new technical regulations calling for flat-bottomed cars from the start of 1983 produced a variety of approaches, Brabham and Ferrari differing, for example, over the aerodynamic validity of long side pods. The ATS, although never a winner, is significant as the first carbon-fibre monocoque without separate upper bodywork. The Ferrari C3 marks Maranello's switch to carbon-fibre technology, although broadly the chassis configuration followed that of the aluminium honeycomb C2 which it superseded in the middle of the year.

Brabham BT52–BMW

Chassis: outer panelling in aluminium, inner panels in carbon fibre. Ultra-slim monocoque to fit new flat-bottom regulations with radiators and intercoolers in tiny side pods, positioned well to the rear.

Suspension: double wishbones front and rear with pushrod activation of inboard spring/dampers.

Engine: BMW M12/13 1½-litre single turbo four cylinder.

Transmission: Brabham/Hewland/Weismann/Alfa Romeo/Getrag, five or six speeds.

Ferrari 126C3

Chassis: carbon-fibre composite monocoque fully enclosing area above driver's legs. Side pods containing water radiators/turbo intercoolers.

Suspension: double wishbones all round with pullrod activation of inboard spring/dampers.

Engine: Ferrari 120-degree 1½-litre twin turbo V6.

Transmission: Ferrari transverse, mounted ahead of rear axle-line, now six speeds.

ATS D6–BMW

Chassis: carbon-fibre composite with no separate body top. Half-length side pods containing water radiators/turbo intercoolers.

Suspension: double wishbones all round with pullrod activation of inboard spring/dampers.

Engine: BMW M12/13 1½-litre single turbo four cylinder.

Transmission: ATS casing, Hewland internals, five speeds.

1984

Summary

Carbon-fibre composite chassis manufacture now fast becoming the norm, although most teams still retaining separate upper bodywork for degree of aerodynamic flexibility. Rocker arm front suspension now almost disappeared, although retained on rear of McLaren to aid aerodynamic packaging. Large conventional aerofoils going a long way to regaining downforce lost by outlawing of shaped ground-effect underbody panels at the start of the 1983 season.

McLaren MP4/2–TAG

Chassis: carbon-fibre composite monocoque fully enclosing area above driver's legs. Retained long side pods housing turbo intercoolers, oil and water radiators.

Suspension: double wishbones with pushrod activation of inboard spring/dampers at front; rocker arm activation of inboard spring/dampers at rear, with lower wishbone.

Engine: Porsche-made TAG 85-degree 1½-litre twin turbo V6.

Transmission: McLaren casing, Hewland internals, five speeds.

Toleman TG184–Hart

Chassis: carbon-fibre composite, fully enclosing driver's legs. Long side pods enclosing turbo intercooler, oil and water radiators.

Suspension: upper and lower wishbones front and rear, pullrod activation of inboard spring/dampers at front, pushrod at rear.

Engine: Brian Hart 415T monobloc 1½-litre single turbo four cylinder.

Transmission: Toleman casing, Hewland internals, five speeds.

Lotus 95T–Renault

Chassis: carbon-fibre/Kevlar composite monocoque manufactured from single sheet of material folded round internal bulkheads. Retained long side pods enclosing turbo intercoolers, oil and water radiators.

Suspension: double wishbones with pullrod activation of inboard spring/dampers front and rear.

Engine: Renault EF1 1½-litre twin turbo V6.

Transmission: Lotus casing, Hewland internals, five speeds.

1985

Summary

Considerable conformity evident now in basic technical layout with little apparent difference between good and bad chassis in terms of specification. Aerodynamic detail now an absolute top priority and the acceleration of the turbo era now putting an added premium on the engine and its associated electrical/injection/management systems.

Ferrari 156/85

Chassis: carbon-fibre composite, fully enclosing driver's legs, with smaller fuel tank to 220-litre capacity regulations and correspondingly lower rear bodywork. Long side pods enclosing turbo intercoolers, oil and water radiators.

Suspension: upper and lower wishbones with pullrod activation of inboard spring/damper units front and rear.

Engine: Ferrari 120-degree 1½-litre twin turbo V6.

Transmission: Ferrari transverse six-speed, mounted ahead of rear axle-line.

Alfa Romeo 185T

Chassis: carbon-fibre composite monocoque, fully enclosing driver's legs, without separate upper bodywork. Medium length side pods housing turbo intercoolers, oil and water radiators.

Suspension: upper and lower wishbones with pullrod activation of inboard spring/damper units at front, pushrod at rear.

Engine: Alfa Romeo 1½-litre twin turbo V8.

Transmission: Alfa Romeo, five speeds.

Tyrrell 014–Renault

Chassis: carbon-fibre composite, fully enclosing driver's legs. Long side panels to house 'standard' Renault turbo intercooler/radiator package for 'customer' cars.

Suspension: upper and lower wishbones with pullrod activation of inboard spring/damper units front and rear.

Engine: Renault EF4/EF15 1½-litre twin turbo V6.

Transmission: Tyrrell casing, Hewland internals, six speeds.

1986

Summary

Gordon Murray attempted an ambitious route with the low-line Brabham BT55 which was claimed to have 30 per cent less frontal area than the previous season's BT54. The first all-carbon-fibre Brabham monocoque, its over-complexity defeated it. More successful was the conventionally engined Benetton which won the Mexican Grand Prix with the 'upright' BMW engine, while the new Haas team squandered the low-line Ford 120-degree V6 by building a car no smaller than the previous year's Hart-engined machine. Benetton would show them how in 1987 when they had the Ford engine.

Brabham BT55–BMW

Chassis: carbon-fibre composite, ultra-low with driver semi-reclined for smaller frontal area. Full length side pods housing turbo intercoolers, oil and water radiators.

Suspension: upper and lower wishbones with pushrod activation of inboard spring/dampers front and rear.

Engine: BMW M12/13/1 1½-litre single turbo four cylinder especially canted over at 72 degrees for lower installation in chassis.

Transmission: Brabham/Weismann transverse, seven speeds.

Benetton B186–BMW

Chassis: carbon-fibre composite. Full length side pods housing turbo intercoolers, oil and water radiators.

Suspension: upper and lower wishbones front and rear with pullrod activation of inboard spring/dampers at front, pushrod at rear.

Engine: BMW M12/13 1½-litre single turbo four cylinder – 'upright' installation.

Transmission: Benetton casing, Hewland internals, six speeds.

Lola THL2–Ford

Chassis: carbon-fibre composite. Full length side pods housing turbo intercoolers, oil and water radiators.

Suspension: upper and lower wishbones with pushrod activation of inboard spring/dampers front and rear.

Engine: Cosworth-made Ford 120-degree 1½-litre twin turbo V6.

Transmission: FORCE casing, Hewland internals, six speeds.

1987

Summary

The on-paper specification of the Lotus and Williams looks pretty similar, but one of the most crucial differences is the FW11B's reclined driving position and consequent smaller frontal area. In this era of 195-litre fuel consumption races, the smaller the frontal area, the less the drag, the better the fuel consumption at a given power output. With the same engine the Lotus could not compete with the Williams in a straight fight and had the additional weight handicap of its active suspension system. The Ferrari F187 heralded the return to a competitive pitch by Maranello. Cars now very similar in mechanical specification.

Williams FW11B–Honda

Chassis: carbon-fibre composite monocoque with semi-reclined driving position, a refined version of the 1986 FW11. Medium length side pods housing turbo intercoolers, oil and water radiators.

Suspension: upper and lower wishbones with pushrod activation of inboard spring/dampers at front, pullrod at rear.

Engine: Honda RA166E/RA167G 1½-litre twin turbo V6.

Transmission: Williams casing, Hewland internals, six speeds.

Ferrari F187

Chassis: carbon-fibre composite monocoque with no separate upper bodywork. Full length side pods housing turbo intercoolers, oil and water radiators.

Suspension: upper and lower wishbones with pullrod activation of inboard spring/damper units front and rear.

Engine: Ferrari 90-degree 1½-litre twin turbo V6.

Transmission: Ferrari longitudinal six-speed.

Lotus 99T–Honda

Chassis: carbon-fibre/Kevlar monocoque. Full length side pods housing turbo intercoolers, oil and water radiators.

Suspension: upper and lower wishbones with pullrod activation of computer-controlled hydraulic jacks.

Engine: Honda RA166E/RA167G 1½-litre twin turbo V6.

Transmission: Lotus casing, Hewland internals, six speeds.

1988

Summary

Season rich in technical variety as new breed of highly sophisticated naturally aspirated cars make challenge to break turbo supremacy in last year of forced induction engines. Great attention being paid to packaging the car within new dimensions dictated by necessity to have pedals behind front axle-line. Particular variety of approach to gearbox design, although McLaren three-axis transmission purely evolved to gain maximum benefit from lower crankshaft centreline in '88 spec. Honda V6.

McLaren MP4/4–Honda

Chassis: carbon-fibre composite monocoque with reclined driving position for improved aerodynamic penetration. Full length side pods housing turbo intercoolers, oil and water radiators.

Suspension: upper and lower wishbones with pushrod activation of inboard spring/dampers front and rear.

Engine: Honda RA168E 1½-litre twin turbo V6.

Transmission: McLaren/Weismann six-speed, three-axis gearbox.

Williams FW12–Judd

Chassis: carbon-fibre composite monocoque with compact side pods housing water radiator/oil-coolers.

Suspension: Williams reactive computer-controlled system with inboard mounted hydraulic jacks activating pushrods front and rear.

Engine: Judd CV 3.5-litre V8.

Transmission: Williams transverse six-speed, mounted ahead of rear axle-line.

Benetton–Ford/Cosworth

Chassis: carbon-fibre monocoque with small side pods containing water radiators/oil-coolers.

Suspension: upper and lower wishbones front and rear with inboard spring/dampers activated by pushrods.

Engine: Cosworth-made Ford DFR 3.5-litre V8.

Transmission: Benetton longitudinal six-speed, with Hewland internals, mounted ahead of rear axle-line.